The Help America Vote Act

Marie Leary

Robert Timothy Reagan

Federal Judicial Center
2012

This Federal Judicial Center publication was undertaken in furtherance of the Center's statutory mission to develop and conduct research and education programs for the judicial branch. The views expressed are those of the author and not necessarily those of the Federal Judicial Center.

Contents

Introduction 1
Basic Requirements 1
   Title I: Grant Program 2
   Title II: Election Assistance Commission 2
   Title III: Requirements 3
      Section 301: Requirements for Voting Systems 3
      Section 302: Requirements for Provisional Balloting and Voter Information 4
      Section 303(a): Requirements for Computerized Statewide Voter Registration 6
      Section 303(b): Identification Requirements for Voters Who Register by Mail 7
   Title IV: Enforcement 8
Enforcement of HAVA in Federal Courts 9
   Enforcement of HAVA by the U.S. Department of Justice 9
      Section 301 Violations 11
      Section 302 Violations 13
      Section 303 Violations 16
   Private Enforcement of HAVA in Federal Courts 17
      Title I 18
      Section 1983 18
      Supremacy Clause 19
      Ripeness 20
      Laches 21
      Section 301 22
      Section 302 23
      Section 303 26
Enforcement of HAVA in State Courts 30
Conclusion 35
Appendix: Help America Vote Act 36

Introduction

The Help America Vote Act of 2002 (HAVA)[1] was Congress's reaction to issues that arose during the 2000 presidential election and the ensuing controversial Florida recount.[2] President George W. Bush signed HAVA into law on October 29, 2002.

HAVA includes standards for provisional ballots, which help prevent the consequences of erroneous purges of voter registration rolls. Instead of turning away eligible voters, polls permit those whose registrations are in question to cast provisional ballots that are counted if it turns out that they were eligible to vote.[3] HAVA also sets minimum standards for voting equipment used in federal elections.[4]

Basic Requirements

A principal reason for HAVA was "to establish minimum election administration standards for States and units of local government with responsibility for the administration of Federal elections."[5] The Act promoted improvements in election procedures through a grant program, an independent commission, and a set of minimum standards for federal elections.[6]

---

1. Pub. L. No. 107-252, 116 Stat. 1666 (2002), *as amended*, 42 U.S.C. §§ 15301–15545 (2011).

2. *See* Robert Pear, *The 2002 Campaign: Ballot Overhaul*, N.Y. Times, Oct. 17, 2002, at A1.

3. Edward B. Foley, *The Promise and* Problems *of Provisional Voting*, 73 Geo. Wash. L. Rev. 1193 (2005).

4. 42 U.S.C. § 15481.

5. H.R. Rep. No. 107-730, pt. 1, at 67 (2002) (Conf. Rep.), *reprinted in* 2002 U.S.C.C.A.N. 1086, 1086.

6. *See* U.S. Dept. of Justice Civil Rights Division, Voting Section, Statutes We Enforce, justice.gov/crt/about/vot/hava/hava.php; Leonard M. Shambon, *Implementing the Help America Vote Act*, 3 Election L.J. 424, 428–31 (2004); Daniel P. Tokaji, *Early Returns on Election Reform: Discretion, Disenfranchisement, and the Help America Vote Act*, 73 Geo. Wash. L. Rev. 1206, 1214 (2005).

Title I: Grant Program

Title I[7] provided funds to states to improve election administration and replace outdated voting systems. States qualifying for the funds had to ensure that all punch card and lever voting machines were replaced by any 2004 election,[8] although Title I allowed a good cause waiver extending the deadline, originally to 2006 elections,[9] later to the March 2008 primaries,[10] and finally to the 2010 general election.[11]

Title II: Election Assistance Commission

Title II[12] created a new federal agency, the Election Assistance Commission (EAC), to serve as a clearinghouse for information on federal election administration requirements. The EAC has four appointed members and can act only with the approval of three members.[13] Its duties are to develop and adopt voluntary guidelines on provisional voting, statewide voter registration databases, and mail-in registration; to adopt voluntary guidelines on voting equipment; to conduct studies on election administration; and to research methods to improve access for voters with disabilities and those who are not proficient in English.[14] HAVA does not give the EAC authority to "issue any rule, promulgate any regulation, or take any other action which imposes any requirement on any State or unit of local govern-

---

7. 42 U.S.C. §§ 15301–15306.
8. *Id.* § 15302(a)(3)(A).
9. Pub. L. No. 107-252, 116 Stat. 1666, 1671 (2002).
10. U.S. Troop Readiness, Veterans' Care, Katrina Recovery, and Iraq Accountability Appropriations Act, Pub. L. No. 110-28 § 6301, 121 Stat. 112, 171 (2007).
11. Omnibus Appropriations Act, Pub. L. No. 111-8, div. D, § 625, 123 Stat. 524, 678 (2009), 42 U.S.C § 15302(a)(3)(B).
12. 42 U.S.C. §§ 15321–15472.
13. *Id.* § 15328.
14. *Id.* §§ 15322(1) & (3), 15501(a), 15441(a).

ment."[15] HAVA required each state to develop a plan that explains how it will comply with HAVA requirements.[16]

Title III: Requirements

Title III[17] created minimum standards for states to follow in several key areas of election administration. Specifically, Title III contains minimum requirements for the following:

- voting systems (§ 301)
- provisional voting and required information for voters (§ 302)
- computerized state-wide voter registration lists (§ 303(a)) and
- requirements for first-time voters who register by mail (§ 303(b))

Section 301: Requirements for Voting Systems

Section 301[18] clarifies that it does not prohibit jurisdictions from using the same kind of voting equipment that they used in November 2000, as long as the equipment meets the general and basic requirements that the statute imposes on all voting systems.[19] Section 301 required that all voting systems, by January 1, 2006, allow voters to verify their choices, provide voters with an opportunity to correct their choices before their votes are cast, and notify voters of over-votes.[20] This is known as notice or second-chance technology.[21] Jurisdictions using paper-based systems such as punch cards could meet this requirement with a voter education program on how to correct mistakes and the ef-

---

15. *Id.* § 15329.
16. *Id.* § 15403(b).
As required by HAVA, all of the states' plans were submitted to the EAC and published in the Federal Register. *Publication of State Plans Pursuant to the Help America Vote Act*, 69 Fed. Reg. 14,001–15,232 (Mar. 24, 2004).
17. 42 U.S.C. §§ 15481–15502.
18. *Id.* § 15481.
19. *Id.* § 15481(c)(1); *see* Tokaji, *supra* note 6, at 1214–15.
20. 42 U.S.C. § 15481(c)(1).
21. Tokaji, *supra* note 6, at 1215.

fect of over-voting.[22] In addition, HAVA requires the following of all voting systems:

- They must have an audit capacity, and they must produce a permanent paper record that can be used for manual audits.[23]
- They must accommodate people with disabilities and provide "the same opportunity for access and participation (including privacy and independence) as for other voters," such as by providing at least one direct-record electronic unit or other accessible voting machine in each polling place.[24]
- They must allow alternative-language access for people whose primary language is not English.[25]

Section 302: Requirements for Provisional Balloting and Voter Information

"Provisional voting allows citizens whose names do not, for whatever reason, appear on registration lists to cast a conditional ballot."[26] Although some states had used provisional ballots, nationwide use in federal elections was mandated for the first time by section 302(a) of HAVA, effective January 1, 2004.[27] Section 302(a) provides that if an individual appears at a polling place and that individual's name does not appear on the official list of eligible voters for that polling place or an election official asserts that the person is not eligible to vote, and if that individual declares through a written affirmation that he or she is "a

---

22. § 15481(a)(1)(B); see Tokaji, *supra* note 6, at 1215 ("HAVA does *not* require that [paper] voting systems provide actual notice and the opportunity to correct mistakes.").
23. 42 U.S.C. § 15481(a)(2).
24. *Id.* § 15481(a)(3)(A), (B).
25. *Id.* § 15481(a)(4).
26. Tokaji, *supra* note 6, at 1217 (citing 42 U.S.C. § 15482(a)).
27. 42 U.S.C. § 15482(a); Tokaji, *supra* note 6, at 1217 (citing Nat'l Comm'n on Fed. Election Reform, *To Assure Pride and Confidence in the Electoral Process* 35 (2001) (stating that 19 states used provisional voting to comply with the National Voter Registration Act's requirements)).

registered voter in the jurisdiction" in which he or she wishes to vote and is "eligible to vote in that election," then that individual has an automatic right to cast a provisional ballot.[28] Officials are required to follow specific procedures under HAVA's provisional voting provisions:

Notification. An individual whose name does not appear on the voter registration list must be notified that he or she is entitled to cast a provisional ballot.[29]

Affirmation. In order to cast a provisional ballot, the voter must affirm that he or she is (a) registered in the jurisdiction and (b) eligible to vote in the election.[30]

Transmittal. Poll workers must transmit the provisional ballot or the information in the affirmation to the appropriate state or local election official.[31]

Counting. If the election official determines that the individual is eligible to vote, the provisional ballot should be counted.[32]

Confirmation. Election officials must establish a free access system allowing provisional voters to ascertain whether or not their provisional ballots were counted and, if not, the reason why not.[33]

As provided by section 303(b), first-time voters who registered by mail but who have not previously voted in federal elections and who do not present appropriate documentation must be allowed to cast a provisional ballot.[34] Also effective January 1, 2004, section 302(b) requires the public posting of the following at each polling place on election day: a sample ballot, information about the hours the polling place would be open,

---

28. 42 U.S.C. § 15482(a)(1), (2).
29. *Id.* § 15482(a)(1).
30. *Id.* § 15482(a)(2).
31. *Id.* § 15482(a)(3).
32. *Id.* § 15482(a)(4).
33. *Id.* § 15482(a)(5)(B); Tokaji, *supra* note 6, at 1217–18.
34. 42 U.S.C. § 15483(b).

instructions on how to vote and cast a provisional ballot, instructions for mail-in registrants and first-time voters relevant to identification requirement, and general information on voting rights and federal and state law prohibitions against fraud and misrepresentation.[35]

Section 303(a): Requirements for Computerized Statewide Voter Registration

Effective January 1, 2004, but extendable for good cause to January 1, 2006, section 303(a)[36] requires each state to establish a uniform, official, centralized, computerized, statewide voter registration list that must include the name and registration information for every registered voter within each state and assign a unique identifier to each registered voter.[37] In addition, the list is to be coordinated with other agency databases within each state—specifically, records on felons and deaths—and accessible electronically by any election official in the state.[38] HAVA also requires states to maintain the databases by requiring that states ensure that the name of each voter appears on the electronic lists, by eliminating the names of voters who are not registered, and by eliminating duplicate names.[39] For new registration applicants, the application must contain the applicant's driver's license number, or the last four digits of the applicant's Social Security number if the applicant does not have a driver's license.[40] If the applicant has neither, the state is to assign a unique identifying number to the applicant.[41] States' chief election officials are required to establish agreements with their state motor vehicle agencies to match the statewide voter regis-

---

35. Shambon, *supra* note 6, at 430.
36. 42 U.S.C. § 15483(a).
37. *Id.* § 15483(a), (d)(1); *see also* Shambon, *supra* note 6, at 430; Tokaji, *supra* note 6, at 1216.
38. *Id.* § 15483(a)(1)(A).
39. *Id.* § 15483(a)(2)(B); *see also* Tokaji, *supra* note 6, at 1216.
40. 42 U.S.C. § 15483(a)(5)(A).
41. *Id.*

tration database with the information in the motor vehicle authority database to enable both officials to verify the accuracy of the voter registration application information.[42] Likewise, the state motor vehicle authority must enter into an agreement with the Social Security commissioner through which identification numbers can be matched to verify the applicant's name, date of birth, and Social Security number, and to verify whether Social Security records show the applicant as deceased, if the person submits the last four digits of the Social Security number instead of a driver's license number.[43]

Section 303(b): Identification Requirements for Voters Who Register by Mail

Section 303(b),[44] which became effective for the 2004 elections, establishes identification requirements for a narrow category of first-time voter who[45]

- registers to vote in a jurisdiction *by mail* after January 1, 2003[46]
- has not previously voted in the state in an election for federal office or has not previously voted in the jurisdiction, and the jurisdiction is in a state not having a section 303(a) statewide voter list[47]
- has not provided a copy of photo identification or other proof of name and address at the time they mailed in their registration forms[48]

At the time of voting for the first time in person, this voter must present either valid photo identification or a "current utility bill, bank statement, government check, paycheck, or other government document that shows the name and address of the

---

42. *Id.* § 15483(a)(5)(B); *see also* Shambon, *supra* note 6, at 430.
43. *Id.*
44. *Id.* § 15483(b).
45. *Id.* § 15483(b), (d)(1)(A); *see also* Tokaji, *supra* note 6, at 1217.
46. *Id.* § 15483(b)(1)(A).
47. *Id.* § 15483(b); *see also* Shambon, *supra* note 6, at 430.
48. *Id.* § 15483(d)(2)(B).

voter."[49] If voting for the first time by mail, the voter must provide photocopies of these documents.

If the first-time voter does not present proper identification, the person must be allowed to cast a provisional ballot, which then must be verified according to the procedures in section 302 described above.[50] HAVA refers to this procedure as fail-safe voting,[51] which was established so that "citizens who do not bring the proper documentation will nevertheless have their votes counted, if they are in fact eligible to vote."[52] These requirements do not apply to individuals who are entitled to vote absentee under various federal laws such as the Uniformed and Overseas Citizens Absentee Voting Act and the Voting Accessibility for the Elderly and Handicapped Act.[53] In addition, a voter is exempt from the identification requirement if at the time of the mail registration the voter provides the voter's driver's license number or the last four digits of the voter's Social Security number and the identification information is verified through the statewide registration database (i.e., the state is able to match that information with an existing state identification record bearing the same number, name, and date of birth as provided in the registration application).[54]

Title IV: Enforcement

HAVA established two enforcement processes. Under section 401, the Attorney General may file a civil suit against a state seeking declaratory or injunctive relief to carry out the uniform and nondiscriminatory election technology and administration

---

49. *Id.* § 15483(b)(2)(A).
50. *Id.* § 15483(b)(2)(B).
51. *Id.*
52. Tokaji, *supra* note 6, at 1218.
53. Press Release, U.S. Dept. of Justice, *Help America Vote Act of 2002: Provisions Taking Effect January 1, 2004* (Dec. 31, 2003), *available at* justice.gov/opa/pr/2003/December/03_crt_728.htm.
54. 42 U.S.C. § 15483(b)(3)(B); *see also* Press Release, U.S. Dept. of Justice, *supra* note 53.

requirements that apply to all states under HAVA sections 301, 302, and 303.[55] The Attorney General has delegated § 401 enforcement authority to the Voting Section of the Justice Department's Civil Rights Division.[56] In addition to litigation, the Justice Department enforces HAVA through educational campaigns, outlining requirements of HAVA, responding to inquiries from state and local officials about HAVA's requirements, and maintaining a HAVA information page on the internet.[57]

In order to receive HAVA funds from the federal government, section 402 requires states to implement a uniform and nondiscriminatory complaint procedure to address and rectify the complaints of citizens regarding the administration of federal elections.[58] A state finding that there has been a violation "shall provide the appropriate remedy."[59] If the state fails to meet the 90-day deadline for addressing the complaint, the statute provides for a 60-day alternative dispute resolution procedure.[60]

Enforcement of HAVA in Federal Courts

Enforcement of HAVA by the U.S. Department of Justice

Section 401 of HAVA assigns responsibility for bringing claims against states for failure to meet HAVA requirements to the Justice Department. As evidenced by a March 2003 letter of guidance to all states regarding implementation of HAVA provi-

---

55. 42 U.S.C. § 15511.
56. U.S. Dept. of Justice Civil Rights Division Voting Section, *Help America Vote Act—Frequently Asked Questions*, available at justice.gov/crt/about/vot/misc/faq.php.
57. usdoj.gov/crt/voting/hava/have html.
58. 42 U.S.C. § 15512.
59. *Id.*
60. *Id.*

sions[61] and a December 2003 press release offering assistance to any state that "falls short of full implementation,"[62] from the very beginning the Justice Department adopted a policy of reaching out and helping states to become compliant with HAVA through education campaigns and coordinated efforts before resorting to litigation.[63] This approach has provided the Justice Department with the opportunity to determine whether a state simply failed to implement the HAVA mandates or whether the state suffered setbacks in implementation that could be addressed by the Justice Department and the EAC by providing the state with needed information and fund-management resources before taking enforcement actions.[64] The Justice Department's litigation history provides further evidence of this "litigation-as-the-last-resort" approach. Since January 1, 2004, the date that states were to be in compliance with HAVA's requirements governing provisional voting, identification of mail-in voters, provision of voter information, and the establishment of accessible computerized statewide voter registration lists,[65] the Justice Department's Civil Rights Division brought only 12 cases in federal district courts against states for violation of one

---

61. U.S. Dept. of Justice Civil Rights Division Voting Section, Statutes We Enforce: Help America Vote Act of 2002, *available at* usdoj.gov/crt/voting/hava/have html (providing a link to an example of the March 17, 2003, letter sent to the chief election official, governor, and attorney general of each state, the District of Columbia, Guam, American Samoa, the U.S. Virgin Islands, and Puerto Rico).

62. *See* Press Release, U.S. Dept. of Justice, *Justice Department Outlines Strategy for Effective Enforcement of Election Reform Law for 2004* (Dec. 31, 2003), *available at* justice.gov/opa/pr/2003/December/03_crt_727.htm.

63. Tiana Butcher, *Help America Vote Act Enforcement*, 1 Legis. & Pol'y Brief, Fall 2008, at 7.

64. *Id.* at 25.

65. States were permitted to request for good cause a waiver until January 1, 2006, of the requirement to implement a computerized statewide voter registration list. As of December 31, 2003, the Justice Department reported that 37 covered jurisdictions obtained this waiver. *See* Press Release, U.S. Dept. of Justice, *supra* note 62.

or more provisions of HAVA.[66] Most of these cases were resolved by settlements.

Section 301 Violations

Alleged violations of section 301 included failure to comply with voting system standards, failure to ensure full access to voting for disabled voters, and failure to provide certain alternative language information.

United States v. Philadelphia (E.D. Pa. 2:06-cv-4592). The Justice Department filed a federal complaint against Philadelphia under the Voting Rights Act on October 13, 2006, complaining that the city was failing to accommodate Spanish-speaking and disabled voters.[67] On October 25, the Department moved for a temporary restraining order requiring the appointment of observers.[68] A three-judge court heard the motion on November 3—four days before the 2006 general election—and denied immediate relief.[69] The court concluded that the Department had delayed too long in bringing its complaint and motion—it had known most of the relevant facts since July—and the Department's case was weak.[70] On April 26, 2007, the Department filed an amended complaint including HAVA and the National Voter Registration Act as additional authorities for mandated improvements in Philadelphia's accommodation of Spanish-

---

66. U.S. Dept. of Justice Civil Rights Division Voting Section, Cases Raising Claims Under The Help America Vote Act, *available at* justice.gov/crt/about/vot/litigation/recent_hava.php.

67. Complaint, United States v. Philadelphia, No. 2:06-cv-4592 (E.D. Pa. Oct. 13, 2006), D.E. 1.

68. Motion, *id.* (Oct. 25, 2006), D.E. 9.

69. Order, *id.* (Nov. 3, 2006), D.E. 25 (order by Circuit Judge D. Brooks Smith and District Judges Harvey Barttle III and Petrese B Tucker).

70. Opinion, *id.* (Nov. 8, 2006), D.E. 27, *available at* 2006 WL 3922115.

speaking and disabled voters.[71] On the following day, the parties filed a stipulation to dismiss the action as settled.[72]

United States v. Maine (D. Me. 1:06-cv-86). On July 28, 2006, the Justice Department filed a federal complaint alleging that Maine was violating HAVA section 301(a) by not adequately accommodating disabled voters and that Maine was violating both HAVA section 303(a) and the National Voter Registration Act by failing to maintain an adequate statewide voter registration list.[73] With the complaint, the Department filed a proposed consent decree, which Judge John A. Woodcock Jr. signed on August 1.[74] Judge Woodcock approved modifications to the schedule of compliance on October 27, 2006,[75] and April 4, 2007.[76] The consent decree expired on December 31, 2009, and Judge Woodcock determined that no further court oversight was necessary.[77]

United States v. New York (N.D.N.Y. 1:06-cv-263). On March 1, 2006, the Justice Department filed a federal complaint against New York in the Northern District of New York for failure to comply with HAVA section 301 concerning voting mechanisms and failure to comply with HAVA section 303(a) concerning statewide voter registration lists.[78] Three weeks later, Judge Gary L. Sharpe issued a preliminary injunction requir-

---

71. Amended Complaint, *id.* (Apr. 26, 2007), D.E. 35.
72. Stipulation, *id.* (Apr. 27, 2007), D.E. 36; *see* Order, *id.* (June 1, 2007), D.E. 37 (dismissing the action as settled and retaining jurisdiction until July 1, 2009, to enforce the settlement agreement).
73. Complaint, United States v. Maine, No. 1:06-cv-86 (D. Me. July 28, 2006), D.E. 1.
74. Consent Decree, *id.* (Aug. 1, 2006), D.E. 2.
75. Amended Consent Decree, *id.* (Oct. 27, 2006), D.E. 4.
76. Supplemental Consent Decree, *id.* (Apr. 4, 2007), D.E. 7.
77. Notice, *id.* (Feb. 2, 2010), D.E. 8.
78. Complaint, United States v. New York State Bd. of Elections, No. 1:06-cv-263 (N.D.N.Y. Mar. 1, 2006), D.E. 1.

ing New York to submit to the court a plan for compliance.[79] New York's compliance efforts remain underway.[80]

Section 302 Violations

Alleged violations of section 302 included failure to ensure provisional ballots were available and offered to voters, failure to post required information at polling places during federal elections, failure to provide information on the process of casting a provisional ballot, and failure to establish a free access system for voters to ascertain whether their provisional ballots were counted.

United States v. Fort Bend County (S.D. Tex. 4:09-cv-1058). On April 9, 2009, the Justice Department filed a federal civil action in Houston, Texas, claiming that Fort Bend County was (1) violating HAVA by not providing voters with provisional ballots as required and (2) violating the Voting Rights Act by not adequately facilitating voting by Spanish speakers.[81] With the complaint, the government filed an agreed and proposed consent decree.[82] Judge Kenneth Hoyt signed the decree on April 13.[83]

United States v. Bolivar County (N.D. Miss. 2:08-cv-33). The Justice Department filed a federal complaint in the Northern District of Mississippi's Delta Division on February 15, 2008, claiming that Bolivar County failed to provide provisional voters in the 2006 general election with free access to information on whether their votes were counted.[84] The Department filed with its complaint a stipulated and proposed consent de-

---

79. Preliminary Injunction, *id.* (Mar. 23, 2006), D.E. 38.
80. Status Report, *id.* (June 8, 2012), D.E. 438 (178th status report).
81. Complaint, United States v. Fort Bend Cnty., No. 4:09-cv-1058 (S.D. Tex. Apr. 9, 2009), D.E. 1.
82. Proposed Consent Decree, *id.* (Apr. 9, 2009), D.E. 2.
83. Consent Decree, *id.* (Apr. 13, 2009), D.E. 4.
84. Complaint, United States v. Bolivar Cnty., No. 2:08-cv-33 (N.D. Miss. Feb. 15, 2008), D.E. 1.

cree.[85] Judge Neal Biggers signed the consent decree on February 27.[86]

United States v. Galveston County (S.D. Tex. 3:07-cv-377). In the Southern District of Texas's Galveston Division, the Justice Department filed a federal complaint against Galveston County on July 16, 2007, claiming violations of (1) HAVA by failing to properly provide provisional ballots in the 2006 general election and (2) the Voting Rights Act by insufficiently accommodating Spanish-speaking voters.[87] With its complaint, the Department filed a stipulated and proposed consent decree.[88] Judge John D. Rainey signed the decree on July 20.[89]

United States v. Cibola County (D.N.M. 1:93-cv-1134). A 1993 action by the Justice Department under the Voting Rights Act resulted in an order that Cibola County in New Mexico improve its accommodation of voters speaking Keresan and Navajo.[90] On January 31, 2007, the Department filed an amended complaint[91] and a settlement agreement[92] expanding the case to include claims under HAVA with respect to adequate provision of provisional ballots and claims under the National Voter Registration Act.

United States v. Cochise County (D. Ariz. 4:06-cv-304). The Justice Department filed a federal complaint against Cochise County, Arizona, on June 16, 2006, alleging violation of HAVA by failing to post adequate information at the polls and violation

---

85. Proposed Consent Decree, *id.* (Feb. 15, 2008), D.E. 3.
86. Consent Decree, *id.* (Feb. 27, 2008), D.E. 6.
87. Complaint, United States v. Galveston Cnty., No. 3:07-cv-377 (S.D. Tex. July 16, 2007), D.E. 1
88. Proposed Consent Decree, *id.* (July 16, 2007), D.E. 3.
89. Consent Decree, *id.* (July 20, 2007), D.E. 5.
90. Order, United States v. Cibola Cnty., No. 1:93-cv-1134 (D.N.M. May 3, 2004), D.E. 82 (extending order through 2006 elections).
91. Amended Complaint, *id.* (Jan. 31, 2007), D.E. 86.
92. Settlement Agreement, *id.* (Jan. 31, 2007), D.E. 89; *see* Order, *id.* (Mar. 19, 2007), D.E. 91 (three-judge order approving settlement agreement by Circuit Judge Bobby L. Baldock and District Judges John E. Conway and C. LeRoy Hansen).

of the Voting Rights Act by failing to adequately accommodate Spanish-speaking voters.[93] With its complaint, the Department filed a proposed consent decree, which a three-judge court approved on October 12.[94]

United States v. Westchester County (S.D.NY 7:05-cv-650). The Justice Department filed a federal complaint against Westchester County in the Southern District of New York's White Plains courthouse on January 19, 2005, charging that the county failed to provide information at polls required by section 302 of HAVA and failed to accommodate Spanish-speaking voters in violation of the Voting Rights Act.[95] A three-judge court signed the consent decree on July 14.[96] In light of an extension of relevant provisions of the Voting Rights Act until 2032, the Justice Department moved to extend the consent decree until the end of 2008,[97] and the court agreed on December 31 to do that.[98]

United States v. San Benito County (N.D. Cal. 5:04-cv-2056). The Justice Department filed a federal complaint in San Jose, California, on May 26, 2004, against San Benito County for (1) not providing provisional voters with sufficient information about how to find out if their ballots were counted, (2) not providing provisional voters with reasons if their ballots were not counted, both in violation of HAVA section 302, and

---

93. Complaint, United States v. Cochise Cnty., No. 4:06-cv-304 (D. Ariz. June 16, 2006), D.E. 1.

94. Consent Decree, *id.* (Oct. 12, 2006), D.E. 11 (order by Circuit Judge William A. Fletcher and District Judges Frank R. Zapata and Raner C. Collins).

95. Complaint, United States v. Westchester Cnty., No. 7:05-cv-650 (S.D.N.Y. Jan. 19, 2005), D.E. 1.

96. Consent Decree, *id.* (July 14, 2005), D.E. 4 (order issued by Circuit Judge Barrington D. Parker Jr. and District Judges Colleen McMahon and John G. Koeltl).

97. Consent Decree Extension Brief, *id.* (Sept. 5, 2007), D.E. 6.

98. Consent Decree Extension, *id.* (Jan. 3, 2008), D.E. 31 (order issued by Circuit Judge Barrington D. Parker Jr. and District Judges John G. Koeltl and Kenneth M. Karas).

(3) failing to adequately accommodate Spanish-speaking voters, in violation of the Voting Rights Act.[99] With its complaint, the Department filed a stipulated and proposed consent decree.[100] A three-judge court signed the consent decree on October 1.[101]

Section 303 Violations

Alleged violations of section 303 included failure to comply with requirements for a statewide voter registration database and failure to require identification from certain first-time voters who registered by mail.

United States v. Alabama (M.D. Ala. 2: 06-cv-392). Five weeks before Alabama's June 6, 2006, primary election, the Justice Department filed an action alleging Alabama's violation of HAVA section 303 by not maintaining an adequate statewide voter registration list and not updating its mail-in voter registration forms to ensure identification matching for first-time voters.[102] With its complaint, the Department filed a preliminary injunction motion.[103] On May 30, Judge W. Keith Watkins issued a preliminary injunction requiring presentation of a compliance plan by June 29 for review at a July 20 hearing.[104] At the hearing, Judge Watkins ordered compliance by August 31, 2007, in time for the 2008 primary.[105] Because Alabama's secretary of state said that she could not ensure compliance with the court's order, Judge Watkins appointed Alabama's governor

---

99. Complaint, United States v. San Benito County, No. 5:04-cv-2056 (N.D. Cal. May 26, 2004), D.E. 1.

100. Proposed Consent Decree, *id.* (May 26, 2004), D.E. 3.

101. Consent Decree, *id.* (Oct. 1, 2004), D.E. 11 (order issued by Circuit Judge Carlos Bea and District Judges Jeremy Fogel and James Ware).

102. Complaint, United States v. Alabama, No. 2:06-cv-392 (M.D. Ala. May 1, 2006), D.E. 1.

103. Preliminary Injunction Motion, *United States v. Alabama*, No. 2:06-cv-392 (M.D. Ala. May 1, 2006), D.E. 2.

104. Preliminary Injunction at 11, *id.* (June 7, 2006), D.E. 16, *available at* 2006 WL 1598839.

105. Order at 4, *id.* (July 21, 2006), D.E. 38.

as a special master to supervise compliance.[106] On October 24, 2007, Judge Watkins determined that Alabama was in compliance with HAVA.[107] Governor Bob Riley submitted his twenty-first and final status report on August 22, 2008.[108]

United States v. New Jersey (D.N.J. 2:06-cv-4889). On October 12, 2006, the Justice Department filed a federal complaint against New Jersey, claiming that the state was violating both HAVA and the National Voter Registration Act by not maintaining an adequate computerized statewide voter registration list.[109] With the complaint, the Department filed a stipulated order, which Judge Jose L. Linares signed that day.[110]

United States v. New York (N.D.N.Y. 1:06-cv-263). As discussed *supra* under Section 301 Violations, the district court continues to monitor New York's compliance with HAVA section 303(a) concerning statewide voter registration lists.[111]

Private Enforcement of HAVA in Federal Courts

Although HAVA's section 401 assigns enforcement responsibility to the Justice Department, private, nongovernmental litigants have also brought cases in federal courts seeking enforcement of HAVA's requirements, in part because Congress did not give the EAC the authority to promulgate regulations to clarify HAVA's provisions.

Plaintiffs have pursued causes of action under (1) the civil rights section 1983 of the U.S. Code's title 42 and (2) the Supremacy Clause of the U.S. Constitution. In addition to the question of whether the plaintiff has standing, ripeness is often an important issue for the court.

---

106. Special Master Order, *id.* (Aug. 8, 2006), D.E. 64.
107. Final Order and Judgment at 2, *id.* (Sept. 18, 2008), D.E. 160.
108. Final Special Master Status Report, *id.* (Aug. 22, 2008), D.E. 153.
109. Complaint, United States v. New Jersey, No. 2:06-cv-4889 (D.N.J. Oct. 12, 2006), D.E. 1.
110. Stipulated Order, *id.* (Oct. 12, 2006), D.E. 2.
111. Status Report, United States v. New York State Bd. of Elections, No. 1:06-cv-263 (N.D.N.Y. June 8, 2012), D.E. 438 (178th status report).

Title I

The court of appeals for the Second Circuit affirmed a district court's decision that private plaintiffs did not have a private right of action under HAVA's title I.

Loeber v. Spargo (N.D.N.Y. 1:04-cv-1193). In a pro se complaint, 11 plaintiffs characterizing themselves as "Ad Hoc New York State Citizens for Constitutional Legislative Redistricting," filed an October 15, 2004, challenge to the 2002 districting of New York's legislature.[112] Among the plaintiffs' claims was one that the allocation of HAVA funds to New York was improper because it was based on the voting age population instead of the citizen voting age population.[113] Judge Lawrence E. Kahn determined that the plaintiffs did not have standing to challenge the funding scheme,[114] and the court of appeals affirmed.[115]

Section 1983

The Voting Rights Act and the National Voter Registration Act explicitly provide for private rights of action, but HAVA does not.[116] Section 1983, however, provides a right of action against persons acting under the color of state law for redress of a "deprivation of any rights, privileges, or immunities secured by the Constitution and laws."[117]

There are two major limitations on a section 1983 right of action. First, the statutory scheme must not expressly or impli-

---

112. Complaint, Loeber v. Spargo, No. 1:04-cv-1193 (N.D.N.Y. Oct. 15, 2004), D.E. 1.
113. Opinion at 1, *id.* (Jan. 8, 2008), D.E. 81, *available at* 2008 WL 111172.
114. *Id.* at 7–10.
115. Loeber v. Spargo, 391 F. App'x 55 (2d Cir. 2010).
116. Butcher, *supra* note 63, at 14; Daniel P. Tokaji, *Public Rights and Private Rights of Action: The Enforcement of Federal Election Laws*, 44 Ind. L. Rev. 113, 126, 138 (2010).
117. 42 U.S.C. § 1983 (2011).

citly preclude the action.[118] Second, the federal statute relied on must confer an individual right.[119] The second limitation has proved to be the more challenging for HAVA plaintiffs.

The court of appeals for the Sixth Circuit determined that HAVA's provisions for provisional ballots create unambiguous rights for voters enforceable by section 1983.[120] A district court in another circuit came to the same conclusion.[121]

Because HAVA's provisions for provisional ballots are enforceable through section 1983, courts may award attorney fees to successful plaintiffs.[122]

Supremacy Clause

Another basis for private actions to enforce HAVA is the Constitution's Supremacy Clause:

> This Constitution, and the Laws of the United States which shall be made in Pursuance thereof; and all Treaties made, or which shall be made, under the Authority of the United States, shall be the supreme Law of the Land; and the Judges in every State shall be bound thereby, any Thing in the Constitution or Laws of any State to the Contrary notwithstanding.[123]

When the plaintiff brings suit under the Supremacy Clause, the court applies preemption analysis to determine whether Congress may displace, or preempt, state law whenever it intends to and is acting within the scope of its constitutionally enumerated powers. HAVA does not expressly preempt state law, and it clearly does not occupy the field of election law, so

---

118. City of Rancho Palos Verdes v. Abrams, 544 U.S. 113, 120–25 (2005).

119. Gonzaga Univ. v. Doe, 536 U.S. 273, 283–86 (2002).

120. Sandusky Cnty. Democratic Party v. Blackwell, 387 F.3d 565, 572–73 (6th Cir. 2004).

121. Fla. Democratic Party v. Hood, 342 F. Supp. 2d 1073, 1077–78 (N.D. Fla. 2004).

122. *E.g.*, White v. Blackwell, 418 F. Supp. 2d 988 (N.D. Ohio 2006); White v. Blackwell, 409 F. Supp. 2d 919, 923–24 (N.D. Ohio 2006).

123. U.S. Const. art. VI, cl. 2.

the applicable preemption analysis for HAVA cases is conflict preemption.

Courts have found the following HAVA provisions enforceable in private lawsuits under the Supremacy Clause:

- provisional-ballot requirements[124]
- fail-safe provisions for first-time voters who register by mail[125]

Ripeness

Ripeness is an essential requirement of any lawsuit. In the HAVA context, ripeness was more of an issue in advance of HAVA's deadlines.

American Association of People with Disabilities v. Shelley (C.D. Cal. 2:04-cv-1526) and Benavidez v. Shelley (C.D. Cal. 2:04-cv-3318). The district court ruled that an action brought in 2004 by and on behalf of disabled voters pursuant to HAVA's requirement that election procedures accommodate disabled voters was not ripe, because HAVA's requirements for disabled voters would not be in effect until 2006.[126] Judge Florence-Marie Cooper denied the plaintiffs' motion for immediate injunctive relief on other grounds as well.[127] After difficulties emerged in the March 2004 California primary elections, California's secretary of state, in a controversial decision, decertified electronic voting machines in several counties for the 2004 general election, citing security and technological concerns.[128] Disabled voters, their advocates, and Riverside County filed

---

124. Opinion at 7–8, Hawkins v. Blunt, No. 2:04-cv-4177 (W.D. Mo. Oct. 12, 2004), D.E. 65 [hereinafter *Hawkins* Opinion].

125. Wash. Ass'n of Churches v. Reed, 492 F. Supp. 1264, 1269 (W.D. Wash. 2006); League of Women Voters v. Blackwell, 340 F. Supp. 2d 823, 827–28 (N.D. Ohio 2004).

126. Am. Ass'n of People with Disabilities v. Shelley, 324 F. Supp. 2d 1120, 1126–27 (C.D. Cal. 2004).

127. *Id.* at 1125–32.

128. *Id.* at 1124; *see* Seema Mehta & Stuart Pfeifer, *E-Voting: 1 County Sues State*, L.A. Times, May 5, 2004, at 1.

ultimately unsuccessful federal actions challenging the secretary's decertification.[129]

Laches

Election litigation always has some time pressure, because there is always another election on the horizon. In some cases, the time pressure is measured in hours or days. Courts will sometimes take into account whether the action has been filed early enough to permit a reasonable remedy.

Lucas County Democratic Party v. Blackwell (N.D. Ohio 3:04-cv-7646). Eighteen days before the 2004 general election, the Democratic Parties of Ohio and Lucas County filed a federal challenge to instructions provided by Ohio's secretary of state to county boards of elections, alleging that they violated HAVA with respect to a requirement for provision of a driver's license number or the last four digits of a Social Security number when registering to vote at state offices.[130] Sua sponte, Judge James G. Carr denied the plaintiffs a preliminary injunction because "there is not enough time between now and the election to develop the evidentiary record necessary to determine if the plaintiffs are likely to succeed on the merits of their claim" and the plaintiffs did not explain why they waited until so long after the secretary issued his instructions and so close to the 2004 elec-

---

129. *Am. Ass'n of People with Disabilities*, 324 F. Supp. 2d at 1124–25; *see* Docket Sheet, Benavidez v. Shelley, No. 2:04-cv-3318 (C.D. Cal. May 11, 2004); Docket Sheet, Am. Ass'n of People with Disabilities v. Shelley, No. 2:04-cv-1526 (C.D. Cal. Mar. 8, 2004); *see* Hugo Martin & Seema Mehta, *2 Counties, State Reach a Deal on E-Vote Machines*, L.A. Times, July 14, 2004, at 6 (reporting on out-of-court agreements by the parties on some issues).

130. Complaint, Lucas Cnty. Democratic Party v. Blackwell, No. 3:04-cv-7646 (N.D. Ohio Oct. 15, 2004), D.E. 1.

tion to file the suit.[131] The plaintiffs dismissed their action voluntarily in December.[132]

Section 301

Courts have not found private rights of action to enforce HAVA's requirements for voting systems.

Paralyzed Veterans of America v. McPherson (N.D. Cal. 4:06-cv-4670). A district court determined that HAVA's requirement that voting systems be accessible to persons with disabilities was not enforceable by voters.[133] Finding the issue a "close, difficult question," Judge Sandra Brown Armstrong answered the following question in favor of the defendants: "whether the statute unambiguously confers a federal *right*, not merely a benefit to a particular class."[134] The suit was brought on August 1, 2006, by five disabled voters and three organizations supporting disabled persons, claiming both constitutional and HAVA grounds for relief.[135] On October 31, 2008, the plaintiffs notified the court that the last remaining issues of litigation had been settled.[136]

Taylor v. Onorato (W.D. Pa. 2:06-cv-481). Judge Gary L. Lancaster determined that HAVA's requirements for voting systems are not enforceable in private actions.[137] "[A] private right

---

131. Lucas Cnty. Democratic Party v. Blackwell, 341 F. Supp. 2d 861, 863 (N.D. Ohio 2004).

132. Order, *Lucas Cnty. Democratic Party*, No. 3:04-cv-7646 (N.D. Ohio Dec. 30, 2004), D.E. 9.

133. Opinion at 9–16, Paralyzed Veterans of Am. V. McPherson, No. 4:06-cv-4670 (N.D. Cal. Nov. 28, 2006), D.E. 53, *available at* 2006 WL 3462780.

134. *Id.* at 16.

135. Amended Complaint, *id.* (Aug. 3, 2006), D.E. 4; Complaint, *id.* (Aug. 1, 2006), D.E. 1.

136. Settlement Notice, *id.* (Oct. 31, 2008), D.E. 213; *see* Dismissal, *id.* (Nov. 3, 2008), D.E. 214.

137. Taylor v. Onorato, 428 F. Supp. 2d 384, 386–87 (W.D. Pa. 2006).

of action will only be recognized for violations of federal rights not simply federal laws."[138]

Section 302

HAVA's section 302 mandates that a "registered voter in the jurisdiction in which the individual desires to vote" be "permitted to cast a provisional ballot."[139] Several courts have determined that "jurisdiction" means precinct.[140] If a voter arrives at a correct location and is directed to or given a ballot for the wrong precinct by a poll worker, however, the court of appeals for the Sixth Circuit has determined that the voter should not be disenfranchised because of the poll worker's error.[141]

An effective remedy may require the naming of the correct election officials as defendants.

Service Employees International Union v. Husted (6th Cir. 12–3916 and 12–4069; S.D. Ohio 2:12-cv-562). The court of appeals for the Sixth Circuit affirmed an injunction issued by the district court requiring that provisional ballots cast in the wrong precinct because of poll-worker error be counted, so long as the ballots are cast in a correct location.[142]

Janis v. Nelson (D.S.D. 5:09-cv-5019). Judge Karen E. Schreier determined that state officials were not liable for HAVA's requirement that voters be offered provisional ballots if there is uncertainty about their eligibility to vote, because this HAVA requirement is directed in section 302(a)(1) to election officials at polling places.[143] The plaintiffs' complaint was that South Dakota had wrongfully denied them the right to vote in

---

138. *Id.* at 387.
139. 42 U.S.C. § 15482(a)(2).
140. Sandusky Cnty. Democratic Party v. Blackwell, 387 F.3d 565, 568 (6th Cir. 2004); Fla. Democratic Party v. Hood, 342 F. Supp. 2d 1073, 1079–81 (N.D. Fla. 2004).
141. NEOCH v. Husted, 696 F.3d 580, 584 (6th Cir. 2012).
142. *Id.*
143. Opinion at 10–11, Janis v. Nelson, No. 5:09-cv-5019 (D.S.D. Dec. 30, 2009), D.E. 112, *available at* 2009 WL 5216902.

2008 elections; they alleged that although they were convicted felons they had been sentenced only to probation and so their voting rights should not have been abridged.[144] The case was resolved by a settlement agreement.[145]

Broyles v. Texas (5th Cir. 09-20290; S.D. Tex. 4:08-cv-2320). Judge Lee H. Rosenthal determined, "There is no basis to conclude that the provisions of [HAVA's provisional ballot requirements] apply to voting that does not involve elections for Federal office."[146] In an appeal on other grounds, the court of appeals for the Fifth Circuit affirmed.[147] The HAVA claim was one of many brought to challenge a local election to establish a new municipality.[148]

Florida State Conference of the NAACP v. Browning (11th Cir. 07-15932; N.D. Fla. 4:07-cv-402). The court of appeals for the Eleventh Circuit ruled that HAVA did not require Florida to count provisional ballots cast by voters whose voter registrations were not valid because of a mismatch between the identification number provided by the voter at registration and the state's reference database, even if the mismatch arose from state error.[149]

White v. Blackwell (N.D. Ohio 3:04-cv-7689). Judge David A. Katz determined that Ohio was violating HAVA in 2004 and 2005 elections by denying provisional ballots to voters who had

---

144. Amended Complaint, *id.* (Oct. 7, 2009), D.E. 81; Complaint, *id.* (Feb. 18, 2009), D.E. 1.

145. Dismissal, *id.* (June 1, 2010), D.E. 148; Settlement Agreement, *id.* (May 26, 2010), D.E. 143.

146. Broyles v. Texas, 618 F. Supp. 2d 661, 692–93 (S.D. Tex. 2009).

147. Broyles v. Texas, 381 F. App'x 370 (5th Cir. 2010).

148. Complaint, Broyles v. Texas, No. 4:08-cv-2320 (S.D. Tex. July 25, 2008), D.E. 1.

149. Fla. State Conference of the NAACP v. Browning, 522 F.3d 1153, 1170–71 (11th Cir. 2008).

applied for but who had not cast absentee ballots, even if the voters never received the absentee ballots.[150]

Sandusky County Democratic Party v. Blackwell (6th Cir. 04-4265 and 04-4266; N.D. Ohio 3:04-cv-7582), Bay County Democratic Party v. Land (6th Cir. 04-2307; E.D. Mich. 1:04-cv-10257), and Michigan State Conference of NAACP Branches v. Land (6th Cir. 04-2318; E.D. Mich. 1:04-cv-10267). The court of appeals reversed a district court order requiring Ohio to count provisional ballots so long as they were cast in the right county.

> [W]e hold that ballots cast in a precinct where the voter does not reside and which would be invalid under state law for that reason are not required by HAVA to be considered legal votes.
>
> To hold otherwise would interpret Congress's reasonably clear procedural language to mean that political parties would now be authorized to marshal their supporters at the last minute from shopping centers, office buildings, or factories, and urge them to vote at whatever polling place happened to be handy, all in the effort to turn out every last vote regardless of state law and historical practice. We do not believe that Congress quietly worked such a revolution in America's voting procedures, and we will not order it.[151]

On the same day, the court of appeals also reversed a district court order that provisional ballots in Michigan be counted so long as they are cast in the correct city, village, or township.[152]

Florida Democratic Party v. Hood (N.D. Fla. 4:04-cv-395). Judge Robert L. Hinkle determined that Florida's requirement

---

150. White v. Blackwell, 409 F. Supp. 2d 919, 920–24 (N.D. Ohio 2006); Temporary Restraining Order, White v. Blackwell, No. 3:04-cv-7689 (N.D. Ohio Nov. 2, 2004), D.E. 4.

151. Sandusky Cnty. Democratic Party v. Blackwell, 387 F.3d 565, 568 (6th Cir. 2004).

152. Order, Michigan State Conference of NAACP Branches v. Land, Nos. 04-2307 and 04-2318 (6th Cir. Oct. 26, 2004), *filed as* Order, Bay Cnty. Democratic Party v. Land, No. 1:04-cv-10257 (E.D. Mich. Nov. 15, 2004), D.E. 68.

that provisional ballots must be cast in the correct precinct to be counted did not violate HAVA.[153] Florida's Democratic Party had standing to bring the action on behalf of its members, but the court determined the core claim to be without merit.[154]

Hawkins v. Blunt (W.D. Mo. 2:04-cv-4177). Judge Richard E. Dorr determined that a Missouri statute requiring election officials to refer a voter who arrives at the wrong polling location to the correct location or a central location was not preempted by HAVA.[155] After primary elections in August 2004, three Kansas City voters who voted at incorrect locations sued to have their provisional ballots counted.[156] Following the filing of their complaint, the Kansas City Board of Election Commissioners agreed to count their ballots, and the ballots of others similarly situated, because there was no evidence that the voters had been directed to correct polling locations, as required by Missouri's statute.[157]

Section 303

Some federal actions have challenged state laws and policies as in violation of HAVA's specifications for statewide voter registration databases. Whether the states have violated HAVA has required careful conflict preemption analyses.

Janis v. Nelson (D.S.D. 5:09-cv-5019). In an action brought by convicted felons who claimed that they were wrongfully denied the right to vote in 2008 elections because they were sentenced only to probation, the district court rejected the state defendants' argument that only local officials are liable for

---

153. Fla. Democratic Party v. Hood, 342 F. Supp. 2d 1073, 1079–81 (N.D. Fla. 2004).

154. *Id.* at 1078–81.

155. *Hawkins* Opinion, *supra* note 124.

156. *Id.* at 2; Complaint, *Hawkins*, No. 2:04-cv-4177 (W.D. Mo. Aug. 9, 2004), D.E. 1.

157. *Hawkins* Opinion, *supra* note 124, at 2–3.

HAVA's requirement that voter registrations not be canceled wrongfully.[158]

ACLU of New Mexico v. Chavez (10th Cir. 07-2067; D.N.M. 1:05-cv-1136). The court of appeals for the Tenth Circuit reversed an injunction against a requirement of photo identification for voting in municipal elections in Albuquerque, because HAVA only applies to elections for federal offices.[159] The court of appeals also concluded that the district court's injunction on equal protection grounds was in conflict with the Supreme Court's subsequent decision in *Crawford v. Marion County Election Board*.[160]

Ohio Republican Party v. Brunner (U.S. 08A332; 6th Cir. 08-4322; S.D. Ohio 2:08-cv-913). In a one-paragraph decision, the Supreme Court vacated a temporary restraining order issued by a district judge to enforce HAVA, concluding that the plaintiffs "are not sufficiently likely to prevail on the question whether Congress has authorized the District Court to enforce § 303 in an action brought by a private litigant to justify the issuance of a TRO."[161] In an action brought by the Ohio Republican Party and a voter, Judge George C. Smith determined that Ohio's secretary of state was not ensuring that all new voter registrations were being matched to driver's license and Social Security databases before the voters' absentee ballots were counted, and so Judge Smith issued a temporary restraining order, not quite four weeks before the general election, mandating compliance with HAVA.[162] A panel of the court of appeals

---

158. Opinion at 7–10, Janis v. Nelson, No. 5:09-cv-5019 (D.S.D. Dec. 30, 2009), D.E. 112, *available at* 2009 WL 5216902.

159. ACLU of New Mexico v. Santillanes, 546 F.3d 1313, 1325 (10th Cir. 2008).

160. *Id.* at 1319–25; *see* Crawford v. Marion Cnty. Election Bd., 553 U.S. 181 (2008).

161. Brunner v. Ohio Republican Party, 555 U.S. 5, 6 (2008).

162. Ohio Republican Party v. Brunner, 582 F. Supp. 2d 957, 966 (S.D. Ohio 2008).

stayed Judge Smith's order,[163] but the full court of appeals vacated the panel's stay,[164] and then the Supreme Court overruled the court of appeals.[165]

Florida State Conference of the NAACP v. Browning (11th Cir. 07-15932; N.D. Fla. 4:07-cv-402). The court of appeals for the Eleventh Circuit ruled that a Florida statute requiring the state to match a voter's driver's license number or Social Security number to the corresponding database before a voter registration became final was not preempted by HAVA.[166] HAVA's section 303(a)(5)(A) provides that an application for voter registration include (1) the voter's driver's license number, (2) the last four digits of the voter's Social Security number if the voter does not have a driver's license, or (3) a unique voter registration number provided by the state if the voter has neither a driver's license nor a Social Security number. Three advocacy organizations filed a federal complaint and sought an injunction against a Florida statute that makes voter registration contingent on the state's matching the number provided by the voter to the relevant database.[167] Finding that "[a]s a result of natural and expected human errors in data entry and possible computer glitches in the matching process, this law has resulted in more than 14,000 otherwise eligible voters being kept off the voter rolls," the district court issued a preliminary injunction against the statute.[168] The court of appeals reversed the injunction: "Assuming that plaintiffs are right that section 303(a)(5) of HAVA does not impose matching as a requirement of voter registration,

---

163. Opinion, Ohio Republican Party v. Brunner, No. 08-4322 (6th Cir. Oct. 10, 2008).

164. Ohio Republican Party v. Brunner, 544 F.3d 711, 712 (6th Cir. 2008).

165. *Brunner*, 555 U.S. 5.

166. Fla. State Conference of the NAACP v. Browning, 522 F.3d 1153, 1166–72 (11th Cir. 2008).

167. Amended Complaint, Fla. State Conf. of the NAACP v. Browning, No. 4:07-cv-402 (N.D. Fla. Sept. 21, 2007), D.E. 12; Preliminary Injunction Motion, *id.* (Sept. 17, 2007), D.E. 4; Complaint, *id.* (Sept. 17, 2007), D.E. 1.

168. Preliminary Injunction, *id.* (Dec. 18, 2007), D.E. 105.

it also does not seem to prohibit states from implementing it."[169] On remand, the district court determined that the statute was not unconstitutional.[170] Remaining claims were dismissed as settled.[171]

Washington Association of Churches (W.D. Wash. 2:06-cv-726). The district court determined that a Washington statute requiring that a new voter's identification be matched to either the Social Security Administration database or the Department of Licensing database before the person can be registered to vote was preempted by HAVA, which required matching only "as an administrative safeguard for storing and managing the official list of registered voters, and not as a restriction on voter eligibility.[172] Otherwise HAVA would not provide for the assignment of unique identification numbers to voters who do not have Social Security or driver's license numbers.[173] At the litigation's conclusion, the parties stipulated to an award of $575,000 in attorney fees.[174]

League of Women Voters v. Blackwell (N.D. Ohio 3:04-cv-7622). Judge James G. Carr determined that a directive by Ohio's secretary of state was not in conflict with HAVA: first-time voters who registered by mail must provide at the polling place documentary identification, their driver's license number, or the last four digits of their Social Security number.[175]

---

169. *Fla. State Conference of the NAACP*, 522 F.3d at 1168.
170. Fla. State Conference of the NAACP v. Browning, 569 F. Supp. 2d 1237 (N.D. Fla. 2008).
171. Dismissal, *Fla. State Conf. of the NAACP*, No. 4:07-cv-402 (N.D. Fla. Mar. 1, 2010), D.E. 247.
172. Wash. Ass'n of Churches v. Reed, 492 F. Supp. 1264, 1268–70 (W.D. Wash. 2006) (preliminary injunction).
173. *Id.* at 1268.
174. Order, Wash Ass'n of Churches v. Reed, No. 2:06-cv-726 (W.D. Wash. June 15, 2007), D.E. 78.
175. League of Women Voters v. Blackwell, 340 F. Supp. 2d 823 (N.D. Ohio 2004).

Enforcement of HAVA in State Courts

Presented here are summaries of seven cases in which state courts interpreted HAVA. In one case, Arizona's court of appeals found that Arizona is more generous than federal courts in finding private rights of action to enforce HAVA's provisions.[176] In another case, a Colorado trial court came to the same decision as the prevailing federal court view: HAVA does not provide voters with a right to cast provisional ballots in precincts other than their own.[177]

The primary question in the state court cases was whether HAVA preempted state laws and policies. Pennsylvania's supreme court determined that HAVA's deadline for states to establish HAVA-compliant voting systems preempted a statute that required a referendum on changes to voting systems.[178] On the other hand, state courts determined that HAVA does not preempt (1) counting hand-tallied votes according to an intent-of-the-voter standard,[179] (2) allowing 17-year-olds to submit voter registration applications that the state does not process until they are eligible to vote,[180] or (3) a state requirement that signers of a petition to place a name on the ballot provide their correct town or city of residence.[181]

A trial court in New York determined that federal HAVA litigation did not preempt a state court action challenging the

---

176. Chavez v. Brewer, 222 Ariz. 309, 214 P.3d 397, 405–06 (Ariz. App. 2009).

177. Opinion at 18–21, Colorado Common Cause v. Davidson, No. 04CV7709 (Colo. Dist. Ct. Denver Oct. 18, 2004), *available at* 2004 WL 2360485 [hereinafter *Colorado Common Cause* Opinion].

178. Kuznik v. Westmoreland Cnty. Bd. of Comm'rs, 902 A.2d 476 (Pa. 2006).

179. New Mexico *ex rel.* League of Women Voters v. Herrera, 145 N.M. 563, 203 P.3d 94, 97 (N.M. 2009).

180. Edelman v. Washington, 160 Wash. App. 294, 248 P.3d 581 (2011).

181. Stark v. Kelleher, 32 A.D.3d 663, 820 N.Y.S.2d 193 (N.Y. App. Div. 2006).

state's implementation of HAVA as a violation of the state's constitution.[182]

County of Nassau v. New York (N.Y. Sup. Ct. Albany 7193-10). New York's supreme court for Albany County held that a county's suit in state court challenging the state's implementation of HAVA as a violation of the state's constitution was not preempted by federal litigation over the state's compliance with HAVA.[183] Nassau County was unsuccessful in intervening in the federal case to protect its use of lever voting machines.[184] In affirming an injunction against Nassau in the federal action, the U.S. Court of Appeals for the Second Circuit stated, "Nassau has commenced litigation in state court challenging the constitutionality of [New York's Election Reform and Modernization Act of 2005] under the constitution of New York State. Nothing is preventing Nassau from pursuing that litigation."[185] The state court determined, however, that the county did not have the legal capacity to pursue its action against the state.[186]

Edelman v. Washington (Wash. Ct. App. 399954; Wash. Sup. Ct. Thurston 08-2-02317-3). Washington's court of appeals held that it was not a violation of HAVA for Washington's election officials to accept mail-in voter registrations from 17-year-olds and hold them for processing until the voters turned 18.[187] A researcher for the think tank Evergreen Freedom Foundation challenged the Washington policy as, on the one

---

182. Cnty. of Nassau v. New York, 32 Misc. 3d 709, 711, 927 N.Y.S.2d 548 (N.Y. Sup. Ct. 2011).

183. *Id.*

184. United States v. N.Y. State Bd. of Elections, 312 F. App'x 353 (2d Cir. 2008), *aff'g* Minute Order, United States v. N.Y. State Bd. of Elections, No. 1:06-cv-263 (N.D.N.Y. Dec. 20, 2007), D.E. 175; *see* Cnty. of Nassau v. New York, 724 F. Supp. 2d 295, 299 (E.D.N.Y. 2010) (denying removal of the state court action for lack of a federal question).

185. Order, United States v. Nassau Cnty. Bd. of Elections, No. 10-2320 (2d Cir. Sept. 7, 2010); *see Cnty. of Nassau*, 32 Misc. 3d at 710–11, 927 N.Y.S.2d 548.

186. *Cnty. of Nassau*, 32 Misc. 3d at 712–14, 927 N.Y.S.2d 548.

187. Edelman v. Washington, 160 Wash. App. 294, 248 P.3d 581 (2011).

hand, adding registrations to the state database before the registrations were valid and, on the other hand, not processing the registrations expeditiously as required by HAVA.[188] An administrative law judge, the superior court, and the court of appeals all agreed that the registrations were promptly added to the state database, but they were not added as completed registrations until the voters became eligible.[189] The court of appeals also concluded that omission from the registration form of an instruction not to complete the form to persons not presently eligible to register did not violate HAVA because Washington relied on advice from the HAVA-created Election Assistance Commission.[190]

Chavez v. Brewer (Ariz. App. 1 CA-CV 06-0575; Ariz. Sup. Ct. Maricopa CV2006-007000). Arizona's court of appeals held that although HAVA may not afford voters a private right of action in federal courts respecting a county's selection of voting equipment, Arizona voters have a private right of action in Arizona's state courts pursuant to Arizona statutes enacted in compliance with HAVA, because Arizona courts are more generous than federal courts in finding private rights of action whenever the focus of the statute is protecting individual rights.[191]

New Mexico ex rel. League of Women Voters v. Herrera (N.M.). One week before the 2008 general election, New Mexico's supreme court issued a writ of mandamus overturning New Mexico's attorney general's advisory letter nullifying a statutory provision that hand-tallied votes be counted so long as the intent of the voter is clearly discernible.[192] The attorney general

---

188. *Id.* at 299–302, 248 P.3d at 584–85; *see* Richard Roesler, *Group Cites Underage Voting*, Spokane Spokesman-Rev., June 17, 2008, at 1.
189. *Edelman*, 160 Wash. App. at 302–11, 248 P.3d at 585–90.
190. *Id.* at 312–14, 248 P.3d at 590–92.
191. Chavez v. Brewer, 222 Ariz. 309, 214 P.3d 397, 405–06 (Ariz. App. 2009).
192. New Mexico *ex rel.* League of Women Voters v. Herrera, 145 N.M. 563, 203 P.3d 94 (N.M. 2009).

had determined[193] that a subjective intent-of-the-voter standard conflicted with the U.S. Supreme Court's decision in *Bush v. Gore*[194] and with a HAVA requirement: "Each State shall adopt uniform and nondiscriminatory standards that define what constitutes a vote and what will be counted as a vote for each category of voting system used in the State."[195] New Mexico's supreme court determined that the statutory intent-of-the-voter standard "provides sufficient statewide uniformity to comply with both *Bush v. Gore* and the plain language of HAVA."[196]

Stark v. Kelleher (N.Y. App. Div. 3d Dep't 501016). The appellate division of New York's supreme court rejected an argument by an unsuccessful petitioner for a ballot that HAVA's establishment of voter registration databases nullified local requirements that signers of ballot petitions include their correct town or city.[197]

Kuznik v. Westmoreland County Board of Commissioners (Pa. 18 MAP 2006; Pa. Commw. Ct. 18 MD 2006; Pa. C.P. Westmoreland 06CI00058). Pennsylvania's supreme court determined that HAVA preempted a Pennsylvania statute that required popular approval by referendum for a county to adopt an electronic voting system.[198] Pennsylvania's receipt of HAVA funds required it to eliminate its lever voting machines by its first election in 2006, which was a primary election held on May 16.[199] Pennsylvania's secretary of the commonwealth advised county election officials that the HAVA requirement preempted the statutory requirement for replacement of lever

---

193. *League of Women Voters*, 203 P.3d at 96.
194. 531 U.S. 98 (2000).
195. HAVA § 301(a)(6), 42 U.S.C. § 15481(a)(6) (2011).
196. *League of Women Voters*, 203 P.3d at 97.
197. Stark v. Kelleher, 32 A.D.3d 663, 820 N.Y.S.2d 193 (N.Y. App. Div. 2006).
198. Kuznik v. Westmoreland Cnty. Bd. of Comm'rs, 902 A.2d 476 (Pa. 2006).
199. *Kuznik*, 902 A.2d at 480.

voting machines by referendum.²⁰⁰ Voters in Westmoreland County challenged this decision in the county court of common pleas,²⁰¹ and the action was subsequently transferred to the commonwealth court.²⁰² The commonwealth court judge held that HAVA and the referendum requirement were not in conflict, but the election would have to use lever machines for state matters and paper ballots for federal matters.²⁰³ The supreme court held that this result violated unitary voting; instead, HAVA preempted the statutory requirement for a referendum on electronic voting.²⁰⁴

Colorado Common Cause v. Davidson (Colo. Dist. Ct. Denver 04CV7709). Colorado's trial court upheld two statutory provisions and invalidated one in response to a complaint that argued each violated HAVA.²⁰⁵ (1) A state requirement that provisional ballots be cast in the correct precinct did not violate HAVA: "Congress could never have intended by the use of [the] single word ["jurisdiction"] to displace the precinct-based voting system that has been in place in Colorado since its inception."²⁰⁶ (2) A rule that provisional ballots would not be counted if the voter applied for an absentee ballot, even if the voter never cast or even received the absentee ballot, did violate HAVA.²⁰⁷ (3) Expanding voter identification requirements to all

---

200. *Kuznik*, 902 A.2d at 480, 488.
201. Docket Sheet, Kuznik v. Westmoreland Cnty. Bd. of Comm'rs, No. 06CI00058 (Pa. C.P. Westmoreland Jan. 6, 2006); *Kuznik*, 902 A.2d at 480–81.
202. *Kuznik*, 902 A.2d at 481.
203. Opinion, Kuznik v. Westmoreland Cnty. Bd. of Comm'rs, No. 18 MD 2006 (Pa. Commw. Ct. Feb. 13, 2006), *filed as* Ex. 3, Preliminary Injunction Opposition Brief, Taylor v. Onorato, No. 2:06-cv-481 (W.D. Pa. Apr. 25, 2006), D.E. 70 (unsuccessful federal court effort to enjoin electronic voting machines in Allegheny County as in violation of HAVA on a finding by the district judge that HAVA did not provide the plaintiffs with a private right of action); *Kuznik*, 902 A.2d at 480–81, 487–89.
204. *Kuznik*, 902 A.2d at 480, 489–504, 507–08.
205. *Colorado Common Cause* Opinion, *supra* note 177, at 17–22.
206. *Id.* at 18–21.
207. *Id.* at 21–22.

voters and not just first-time voters who registered by mail did not violate HAVA.[208] The defendants decided not to appeal the judge's ruling.[209]

Conclusion

When HAVA was new, the Justice Department enforced its provisions with a few federal court cases, most of which were resolved by settlement. Key issues were compliance with HAVA by the states' registration databases and voting equipment.

A key issue in private enforcement of HAVA is voters' entitlement to cast provisional ballots and whether those ballots will be counted. An important legal question is whether voters must cast provisional ballots in the correct precinct. Federal courts appear to have settled on a determination that HAVA does not relieve voters from casting their votes in the correct precinct, but principles of fairness may relieve voters from disenfranchisement resulting from misdirection by poll workers.

A second key issue in private cases is the extent to which HAVA preempts state laws and policies respecting registration databases, and these cases require careful conflict preemption analyses.

---

208. *Id.* at 18.
209. *See Election Law Ruling Stands Through Nov. 2*, Denver Post, October 21, 2004, at B4.

Appendix: Help America Vote Act (42 U.S.C. §§ 15301–15545)[210]

Subchapter I—Payments to States for Election Administration Improvements and Replacement of Punch Card and Lever Voting Machines[211]

§ 15301. Payments to States for Activities to Improve Administration of Elections

(a) In General

Not later than 45 days after October 29, 2002, the Administrator of General Services (in this subchapter referred to as the "Administrator") shall establish a program under which the Administrator shall make a payment to each State in which the chief executive officer of the State, or designee, in consultation and coordination with the chief State election official, notifies the Administrator not later than 6 months after October 29, 2002, that the State intends to use the payment in accordance with this section.

(b) Use of Payment

(1) In General

A State shall use the funds provided under a payment made under this section to carry out one or more of the following activities:

(A) Complying with the requirements under subchapter III of this chapter.

(B) Improving the administration of elections for Federal office.

(C) Educating voters concerning voting procedures, voting rights, and voting technology.

(D) Training election officials, poll workers, and election volunteers.

(E) Developing the State plan for requirements payments to be submitted under subpart 1 of part D of subchapter II of this chapter.

---

210. Pub. L. No. 107-252, 116 Stat. 1666 (2002), *as amended*.
211. Title I.

(F) Improving, acquiring, leasing, modifying, or replacing voting systems and technology and methods for casting and counting votes.

(G) Improving the accessibility and quantity of polling places, including providing physical access for individuals with disabilities, providing nonvisual access for individuals with visual impairments, and providing assistance to Native Americans, Alaska Native citizens, and to individuals with limited proficiency in the English language.

(H) Establishing toll-free telephone hotlines that voters may use to report possible voting fraud and voting rights violations, to obtain general election information, and to access detailed automated information on their own voter registration status, specific polling place locations, and other relevant information.

(2) Limitation

A State may not use the funds provided under a payment made under this section—

(A) to pay costs associated with any litigation, except to the extent that such costs otherwise constitute permitted uses of a payment under this section; or

(B) for the payment of any judgment.

(c) Use of Funds To Be Consistent with Other Laws and Requirements

In order to receive a payment under the program under this section, the State shall provide the Administrator with certifications that—

(1) the State will use the funds provided under the payment in a manner that is consistent with each of the laws described in section 15545 of this title, as such laws relate to the provisions of this chapter; and

(2) the proposed uses of the funds are not inconsistent with the requirements of subchapter III of this chapter.

(d) Amount of Payment

(1) In general

Subject to section 15303(b) of this title, the amount of payment made to a State under this section shall be the minimum payment amount described in paragraph (2) plus the voting age population proportion amount described in paragraph (3).

(2) Minimum Payment Amount

The minimum payment amount described in this paragraph is—

    (A) in the case of any of the several States or the District of Columbia, one-half of 1 percent of the aggregate amount made available for payments under this section; and

    (B) in the case of the Commonwealth of Puerto Rico, Guam, American Samoa, or the United States Virgin Islands, one-tenth of 1 percent of such aggregate amount.

(3) Voting Age Population Proportion Amount

The voting age population proportion amount described in this paragraph is the product of—

    (A) the aggregate amount made available for payments under this section minus the total of all of the minimum payment amounts determined under paragraph (2); and

    (B) the voting age population proportion for the State (as defined in paragraph (4)).

(4) Voting Age Population Proportion Defined

The term "voting age population proportion" means, with respect to a State, the amount equal to the quotient of—

    (A) the voting age population of the State (as reported in the most recent decennial census); and

    (B) the total voting age population of all States (as reported in the most recent decennial census).

§ 15302. Replacement of Punch Card or Lever Voting Machines

(a) Establishment of Program

(1) In General

Not later than 45 days after October 29, 2002, the Administrator shall establish a program under which the Administrator shall make a payment to each State eligible under subsection (b) of this section in which a precinct within that State used a punch card voting system or a lever voting system to administer the regularly scheduled general election for Federal office held in November 2000 (in this section referred to as a "qualifying precinct").

(2) Use of Funds

A State shall use the funds provided under a payment under this section (either directly or as reimbursement, including as reimbursement for costs incurred on or after January 1, 2001, under multiyear contracts) to replace punch card voting systems or lever voting systems (as the case may be) in qualifying precincts within that State with a voting system (by purchase, lease, or such other arrangement as may be appropriate) that—

    (A) does not use punch cards or levers;

    (B) is not inconsistent with the requirements of the laws described in section 15545 of this title; and

    (C) meets the requirements of section 15481 of this title.

(3) Deadline

(A) In General

Except as provided in subparagraph (B), a State receiving a payment under the program under this section shall ensure that all of the punch card voting systems or lever voting systems in the qualifying precincts within that State have been replaced in time for the regularly scheduled general election for Federal office to be held in November 2004.

(B) Waiver

If a State certifies to the Administrator not later than January 1, 2004, that the State will not meet the deadline described in subparagraph (A) for good cause and includes in the certification the reasons for the failure to meet such deadline, the State shall ensure that all of the punch card voting systems or lever voting systems in the qualifying precincts within that State will be replaced in time for the first election for Federal office held after November 1, 2010.[212]

---

212. The U.S. Troop Readiness, Veterans' Care, Katrina Recovery, and Iraq Accountability Appropriations Act of 2007, Pub. L. 110-28, 121 Stat. 111, 171, substituted "March 1, 2008" for "January 1, 2006." The Omnibus Appropriations Act of 2009, Pub. L. 111-8, 123 Stat. 523, 678, substituted "November 1, 2010" for "March 1, 2008."

(b) Eligibility

(1) In general

A State is eligible to receive a payment under the program under this section if it submits to the Administrator a notice not later than the date that is 6 months after October 29, 2002 (in such form as the Administrator may require) that contains—

(A) certifications that the State will use the payment (either directly or as reimbursement, including as reimbursement for costs incurred on or after January 1, 2001, under multiyear contracts) to replace punch card voting systems or lever voting systems (as the case may be) in the qualifying precincts within the State by the deadline described in subsection (a)(3) of this section;

(B) certifications that the State will continue to comply with the laws described in section 15545 of this title;

(C) certifications that the replacement voting systems will meet the requirements of section 15481 of this title; and

(D) such other information and certifications as the Administrator may require which are necessary for the administration of the program.

(2) Compliance of States That Require Changes to State Law

In the case of a State that requires State legislation to carry out an activity covered by any certification submitted under this subsection, the State shall be permitted to make the certification notwithstanding that the legislation has not been enacted at the time the certification is submitted and such State shall submit an additional certification once such legislation is enacted.

(c) Amount of Payment

(1) In General

Subject to paragraph (2) and section 15303(b) of this title, the amount of payment made to a State under the program under this section shall be equal to the product of—

(A) the number of the qualifying precincts within the State; and

(B) $4,000.

(2) Reduction

If the amount of funds appropriated pursuant to the authority of section 15304(a)(2) of this title is insufficient to ensure that each State receives the amount of payment calculated under paragraph (1), the Administrator shall reduce the amount specified in paragraph (1)(B) to ensure that the entire amount appropriated under such section is distributed to the States.

(d) Repayment of Funds for Failure to Meet Deadlines

(1) In General

If a State receiving funds under the program under this section fails to meet the deadline applicable to the State under subsection (a)(3) of this section, the State shall pay to the Administrator an amount equal to the noncompliant precinct percentage of the amount of the funds provided to the State under the program.

(2) Noncompliant Precinct Percentage Defined

In this subsection, the term "noncompliant precinct percentage" means, with respect to a State, the amount (expressed as a percentage) equal to the quotient of—

    (A) the number of qualifying precincts within the State for which the State failed to meet the applicable deadline; and

    (B) the total number of qualifying precincts in the State.

(e) Punch Card Voting System Defined

For purposes of this section, a "punch card voting system" includes any of the following voting systems:

    (1) C.E.S.
    (2) Datavote.
    (3) PBC Counter.
    (4) Pollstar.
    (5) Punch Card.
    (6) Vote Recorder.
    (7) Votomatic.

§ 15303. Guaranteed Minimum Payment Amount

(a) In General

In addition to any other payments made under this subchapter, the Administrator shall make a payment to each State to which a payment is made under either section 15301 or 15302 of this title and with respect to which the aggregate amount paid under such sections is less than $5,000,000 in an amount equal to the difference between the aggregate amount paid to the State under sections 15301 and 15302 of this title and $5,000,000. In the case of the Commonwealth of Puerto Rico, Guam, American Samoa, and the United States Virgin Islands, the previous sentence shall be applied as if each reference to "$5,000,000" were a reference to "$1,000,000".

(b) Pro Rata Reductions

The Administrator shall make such pro rata reductions to the amounts described in sections 15301(d) and 15302(c) of this title as are necessary to comply with the requirements of subsection (a) of this section.

§ 15304. Authorization of Appropriations

(a) In General

There are authorized to be appropriated for payments under this subchapter $650,000,000, of which—

> (1) 50 percent shall be for payments under section 15301 of this title; and
>
> (2) 50 percent shall be for payments under section 15302 of this title.

(b) Continuing Availability of Funds After Appropriation

Any payment made to a State under this subchapter shall be available to the State without fiscal year limitation (subject to subsection (c)(2)(B) of this section).

(c) Use of Returned Funds and Funds Remaining Unexpended for Requirements Payments

> *(1) In General*
>
> The amounts described in paragraph (2) shall be transferred to the Election Assistance Commission (established under subchapter II of this chapter) and used by the Commission to make requirements payments under subpart 1 of part D of subchapter II of this chapter.
>
> *(2) Amounts Described*
>
> The amounts referred to in this paragraph are as follows:
>
>> (A) Any amounts paid to the Administrator by a State under section 15302(d)(1) of this title.

(B) Any amounts appropriated for payments under this subchapter which remain unobligated as of September 1, 2003.

(d) Deposit of Amounts in State Election Fund

When a State has established an election fund described in section 15404(b) of this title, the State shall ensure that any funds provided to the State under this subchapter are deposited and maintained in such fund.

(e) Authorization of Appropriations for Administrator

In addition to the amounts authorized under subsection (a) of this section, there are authorized to be appropriated to the Administrator such sums as may be necessary to administer the programs under this subchapter.

§ 15305. Administration of Programs

In administering the programs under this subchapter, the Administrator shall take such actions as the Administrator considers appropriate to expedite the payment of funds to States.

§ 15306. Effective Date

The Administrator shall implement the programs established under this subchapter in a manner that ensures that the Administrator is able to make payments under the program not later than the expiration of the 45-day period which begins on October 29, 2002.

Subchapter II—Commission[213]

Part A—Establishment and General Organization

Subpart 1—Election Assistance Commission

§ 15321. Establishment

There is hereby established as an independent entity the Election Assistance Commission (hereafter in this subchapter referred to as the "Commission"), consisting of the members appointed under this subpart. Additionally, there is established the Election Assistance Commission Standards Board (including the Executive Board of such Board) and the Election Assistance Commission Board of Advisors

---

213. Title II.

under subpart 2 of this part (hereafter in this subpart referred to as the "Standards Board" and the "Board of Advisors", respectively) and the Technical Guidelines Development Committee under subpart 3 of this part.

§ 15322. Duties

The Commission shall serve as a national clearinghouse and resource for the compilation of information and review of procedures with respect to the administration of Federal elections by—

    (1) carrying out the duties described in subpart 3 of this part (relating to the adoption of voluntary voting system guidelines), including the maintenance of a clearinghouse of information on the experiences of State and local governments in implementing the guidelines and in operating voting systems in general;

    (2) carrying out the duties described in part B of this subchapter (relating to the testing, certification, decertification, and recertification of voting system hardware and software);

    (3) carrying out the duties described in part C of this subchapter (relating to conducting studies and carrying out other activities to promote the effective administration of Federal elections);

    (4) carrying out the duties described in part D of this subchapter (relating to election assistance), and providing information and training on the management of the payments and grants provided under such part;

    (5) carrying out the duties described in part B of subchapter III of this chapter (relating to the adoption of voluntary guidance); and

    (6) developing and carrying out the Help America Vote College Program under subchapter V of this chapter.

§ 15323. Membership and Appointment

(a) Membership

  (1) In General

The Commission shall have four members appointed by the President, by and with the advice and consent of the Senate.

  (2) Recommendations

Before the initial appointment of the members of the Commission and before the appointment of any individual to fill a vacancy on the Commission, the Majority Leader of the Senate, the Speaker of the House of Representatives, the Minority Leader of the Senate, and the Minority Leader of the House of Representatives shall each submit to the President a candidate recommendation with respect to each vacancy on the Commission affiliated with the political party of the Member of Congress involved.

(3) Qualifications

Each member of the Commission shall have experience with or expertise in election administration or the study of elections.

(4) Date of Appointment

The appointments of the members of the Commission shall be made not later than 120 days after October 29, 2002.

(b) Term of Service

(1) In General

Except as provided in paragraphs (2) and (3), members shall serve for a term of 4 years and may be reappointed for not more than one additional term.

(2) Terms of Initial Appointees

As designated by the President at the time of nomination, of the members first appointed—

> (A) two of the members (not more than one of whom may be affiliated with the same political party) shall be appointed for a term of 2 years; and
>
> (B) two of the members (not more than one of whom may be affiliated with the same political party) shall be appointed for a term of 4 years.

(3) Vacancies

(A) In General

A vacancy on the Commission shall be filled in the manner in which the original appointment was made and shall be subject to any conditions which applied with respect to the original appointment.

(B) Expired Terms

A member of the Commission shall serve on the Commission after the expiration of the member's term until the successor of such member has taken office as a member of the Commission.

(C) Unexpired Terms

An individual appointed to fill a vacancy shall be appointed for the unexpired term of the member replaced.

(c) Chair and Vice Chair

(1) In General

The Commission shall select a chair and vice chair from among its members for a term of 1 year, except that the chair and vice chair may not be affiliated with the same political party.

(2) Number of Terms

A member of the Commission may serve as the chairperson and vice chairperson for only 1 term each during the term of office to which such member is appointed.

(d) Compensation

(1) In General

Each member of the Commission shall be compensated at the annual rate of basic pay prescribed for level IV of the Executive Schedule under section 5315 of title 5.

(2) Other Activities

No member appointed to the Commission under subsection (a) of this section may engage in any other business, vocation, or employment while serving as a member of the Commission and shall terminate or liquidate such business, vocation, or employment before sitting as a member of the Commission.

§ 15324. Staff

(a) Executive Director, General Counsel, and Other Staff

(1) Executive Director

The Commission shall have an Executive Director, who shall be paid at a rate not to exceed the rate of basic pay for level V of the Executive Schedule under section 5316 of title 5.

(2) Term of Service for Executive Director

The Executive Director shall serve for a term of 4 years. An Executive Director may serve for a longer period only if reappointed for an additional term or terms by a vote of the Commission.

(3) Procedure for Appointment

(A) In General

When a vacancy exists in the position of the Executive Director, the Standards Board and the Board of Advisors shall each appoint a search committee to recommend at least three nominees for the position.

(B) Requiring Consideration of Nominees

Except as provided in subparagraph (C), the Commission shall consider the nominees recommended by the Standards Board and the Board of Advisors in appointing the Executive Director.

(C) Interim Service of General Counsel

If a vacancy exists in the position of the Executive Director, the General Counsel of the Commission shall serve as the acting Executive Director until the Commission appoints a new Executive Director in accordance with this paragraph.

(D) Special Rules for Interim Executive Director

(i) Convening of search committees The Standards Board and the Board of Advisors shall each appoint a search committee and recommend nominees for the position of Executive Director in accordance with subparagraph (A) as soon as practicable after the appointment of their members.

(ii) Interim initial appointment Notwithstanding subparagraph (B), the Commission may appoint an individual to serve as an interim Executive Director prior to the recommendation of nominees for the position by the Standards Board or the Board of Advisors, except that such individual's term of service may not exceed 6 months. Nothing in the previous sentence may be construed to prohibit the individual serving as the interim Executive Director from serving any additional term.

(4) General Counsel

The Commission shall have a General Counsel, who shall be appointed by the Commission and who shall serve under the Executive Director. The General Counsel shall serve for a term of 4 years, and may serve for a longer period only if reappointed for an additional term or terms by a vote of the Commission.

(5) Other Staff

Subject to rules prescribed by the Commission, the Executive Director may appoint and fix the pay of such additional personnel as the Executive Director considers appropriate.

(6) Applicability of Certain Civil Service Laws

The Executive Director, General Counsel, and staff of the Commission may be appointed without regard to the provisions of title 5 governing appointments in the competitive service, and may be paid without regard to the provisions of chapter 51 and subchapter III of chapter 53 of that title relating to classification and General Schedule pay rates, except that an individual so appointed may not receive pay in excess of the annual rate of basic pay for level V of the Executive Schedule under section 5316 of that title.

(b) Experts and Consultants

Subject to rules prescribed by the Commission, the Executive Director may procure temporary and intermittent services under section 3109(b) of title 5 by a vote of the Commission.

(c) Staff of Federal Agencies

Upon request of the Commission, the head of any Federal department or agency may detail, on a reimbursable basis, any of the personnel of that department or agency to the Commission to assist it in carrying out its duties under this chapter.

(d) Arranging for Assistance for Board of Advisors and Standards Board

At the request of the Board of Advisors or the Standards Board, the Commission may enter into such arrangements as the Commission considers appropriate to make personnel available to assist the Boards with carrying out their duties under this subchapter (including contracts with private individuals for providing temporary personnel services or the temporary detailing of personnel of the Commission).

(e) Consultation with Board of Advisors and Standards Board on Certain Matters

In preparing the program goals, long-term plans, mission statements, and related matters for the Commission, the Executive Director and staff of the Commission shall consult with the Board of Advisors and the Standards Board.

§ 15325. Powers

(a) Hearings and Sessions

The Commission may hold such hearings for the purpose of carrying out this chapter, sit and act at such times and places, take such testimony, and receive such evidence as the Commission considers advisable to carry out this chapter. The Commission may administer oaths and affirmations to witnesses appearing before the Commission.

(b) Information from Federal Agencies

The Commission may secure directly from any Federal department or agency such information as the Commission considers necessary to carry out this chapter. Upon request of the Commission, the head of such department or agency shall furnish such information to the Commission.

(c) Postal Services

The Commission may use the United States mails in the same manner and under the same conditions as other departments and agencies of the Federal Government.

(d) Administrative Support Services

Upon the request of the Commission, the Administrator of General Services shall provide to the Commission, on a reimbursable basis, the administrative support services that are necessary to enable the Commission to carry out its duties under this chapter.

(e) Contracts

The Commission may contract with and compensate persons and Federal agencies for supplies and services without regard to section 6101 of title 41.

§ 15326. Dissemination of Information

In carrying out its duties, the Commission shall, on an ongoing basis, disseminate to the public (through the Internet, published reports, and such other methods as the Commission considers appropriate) in a manner that is consistent with the requirements of chapter 19 of title 44 information on the activities carried out under this chapter.

§ 15327. Annual Report

Not later than January 31 of each year (beginning with 2004), the Commission shall submit a report to the Committee on House Administration of the House of Representatives and the Committee on Rules and Administration of the Senate detailing its activities during the fiscal year which ended on September 30 of the previous calendar year, and shall include in the report the following information:

(1) A detailed description of activities conducted with respect to each program carried out by the Commission under this chapter, including information on each grant or other payment made under such programs.

(2) A copy of each report submitted to the Commission by a recipient of such grants or payments which is required under such a program, including reports submitted by States receiving requirements payments under subpart 1 of part D of this subchapter, and each other report submitted to the Commission under this chapter.

(3) Information on the voluntary voting system guidelines adopted or modified by the Commission under subpart 3 of this part and information on the voluntary guidance adopted under part B of subchapter III of this chapter.

(4) All votes taken by the Commission.

(5) Such other information and recommendations as the Commission considers appropriate.

§ 15328. Requiring Majority Approval for Actions

Any action which the Commission is carried out only with the approval of at least three of its members.

§ 15329. Limitation on Rulemaking Authority

The Commission shall not have any authority to issue any rule, promulgate any regulation, or take any other action which imposes any requirement on any State or unit of local government, except to the extent permitted under section 1973gg–7(a) of this title.

§ 15330. Authorization of Appropriations

In addition to the amounts authorized for payments and grants under this subchapter and the amounts authorized to be appropriated for the program under section 15523 of this title, there are authorized to be appropriated for each of the fiscal years 2003 through 2005 such sums as may be necessary (but not to exceed $10,000,000 for each such year) for the Commission to carry out this subchapter.

Subpart 2—Election Assistance Commission Standards Board and Board of Advisors

§ 15341. Establishment

There are hereby established the Election Assistance Commission Standards Board (hereafter in this subchapter referred to as the "Standards Board") and the Election Assistance Commission Board of Advisors (hereafter in this subchapter referred to as the "Board of Advisors").

§ 15342. Duties

The Standards Board and the Board of Advisors shall each, in accordance with the procedures described in subpart 3 of this part, review the voluntary voting system guidelines under such subpart, the voluntary guidance under subchapter III of this chapter, and the best practices recommendations contained in the report submitted under section 15382(b) of this title.

§ 15343. Membership of Standards Board

(a) Composition

(1) In General

Subject to certification by the chair of the Federal Election Commission under subsection (b) of this section, the Standards Board shall be composed of 110 members as follows:

(A) Fifty-five shall be State election officials selected by the chief State election official of each State.

(B) Fifty-five shall be local election officials selected in accordance with paragraph (2).

(2) List of Local Election Officials

Each State's local election officials, including the local election officials of Puerto Rico and the United States Virgin Islands, shall select (under a process supervised by the chief election official of the State) a representative local election official from the State for purposes of paragraph (1)(B). In the case of the District of Columbia, Guam, and American Samoa, the chief election official shall establish a procedure for selecting an individual to serve as a local election official for purposes of such paragraph, except that under such a procedure the individual selected may not be a member of the same political party as the chief election official.

(3) Requiring Mix of Political Parties Represented

The two members of the Standards Board who represent the same State may not be members of the same political party.

(b) Procedures for Notice and Certification of Appointment

(1) Notice to Chair of Federal Election Commission

Not later than 90 days after October 29, 2002, the chief State election official of the State shall transmit a notice to the chair of the Federal Election Commission containing—

    (A) the name of the State election official who agrees to serve on the Standards Board under this subchapter; and

    (B) the name of the representative local election official from the State selected under subsection (a)(2) of this section who agrees to serve on the Standards Board under this subchapter.

(2) Certification

Upon receiving a notice from a State under paragraph (1), the chair of the Federal Election Commission shall publish a certification that the selected State election official and the representative local election official are appointed as members of the Standards Board under this subchapter.

(3) Effect of Failure to Provide Notice

If a State does not transmit a notice to the chair of the Federal Election Commission under paragraph (1) within the deadline described in such paragraph, no representative from the State may

The Help America Vote Act

participate in the selection of the initial Executive Board under subsection (c) of this section.

(4) Role of Commission

Upon the appointment of the members of the Election Assistance Commission, the Election Assistance Commission shall carry out the duties of the Federal Election Commission under this subsection.

(c) Executive Board

(1) In General

Not later than 60 days after the last day on which the appointment of any of its members may be certified under subsection (b) of this section, the Standards Board shall select nine of its members to serve as the Executive Board of the Standards Board, of whom—

    (A) not more than five may be State election officials;
    (B) not more than five may be local election officials; and
    (C) not more than five may be members of the same political party.

(2) Terms

Except as provided in paragraph (3), members of the Executive Board of the Standards Board shall serve for a term of 2 years and may not serve for more than 3 consecutive terms.

(3) Staggering of Initial Terms

Of the members first selected to serve on the Executive Board of the Standards Board—

    (A) three shall serve for 1 term;
    (B) three shall serve for 2 consecutive terms; and
    (C) three shall serve for 3 consecutive terms, as determined by lot at the time the members are first appointed.

(4) Duties

In addition to any other duties assigned under this subchapter, the Executive Board of the Standards Board may carry out such duties of the Standards Board as the Standards Board may delegate.

§ 15344. Membership of Board of Advisors

(a) In General

The Board of Advisors shall be composed of 37 members appointed as follows:

(1) Two members appointed by the National Governors Association.

(2) Two members appointed by the National Conference of State Legislatures.

(3) Two members appointed by the National Association of Secretaries of State.

(4) Two members appointed by the National Association of State Election Directors.

(5) Two members appointed by the National Association of Counties.

(6) Two members appointed by the National Association of County Recorders, Election Administrators, and Clerks.

(7) Two members appointed by the United States Conference of Mayors.

(8) Two members appointed by the Election Center.

(9) Two members appointed by the International Association of County Recorders, Election Officials, and Treasurers.

(10) Two members appointed by the United States Commission on Civil Rights.

(11) Two members appointed by the Architectural and Transportation Barrier 3 Compliance Board under section 792 of title 29.

(12) The chief of the Office of Public Integrity of the Department of Justice,4 or the chief's designee.

(13) The chief of the Voting Section of the Civil Rights Division of the Department of Justice or the chief's designee.

(14) The director of the Federal Voting Assistance Program of the Department of Defense.

(15) Four members representing professionals in the field of science and technology, of whom—

(A) one each shall be appointed by the Speaker and the Minority Leader of the House of Representatives; and

(B) one each shall be appointed by the Majority Leader and the Minority Leader of the Senate.

(16) Eight members representing voter interests, of whom—

(A) four members shall be appointed by the Committee on House Administration of the House of Representatives, of whom two shall be appointed by the chair and two shall be appointed by the ranking minority member; and

(B) four members shall be appointed by the Committee on Rules and Administration of the Senate, of whom two shall be appointed by the chair and two shall be appointed by the ranking minority member.

(b) Manner of Appointments

Appointments shall be made to the Board of Advisors under subsection (a) of this section in a manner which ensures that the Board of Advisors will be bipartisan in nature and will reflect the various geographic regions of the United States.

(c) Term of Service; Vacancy

Members of the Board of Advisors shall serve for a term of 2 years, and may be reappointed. Any vacancy in the Board of Advisors shall be filled in the manner in which the original appointment was made.

(d) Chair

The Board of Advisors shall elect a Chair from among its members.

§ 15345. Powers of Boards; No Compensation for Service

(a) Hearings and Sessions

(1) In General

To the extent that funds are made available by the Commission, the Standards Board (acting through the Executive Board) and the Board of Advisors may each hold such hearings for the purpose of carrying out this chapter, sit and act at such times and places, take such testimony, and receive such evidence as each such Board considers advisable to carry out this subchapter, except that the Boards may not issue subpoenas requiring the attendance and testimony of witnesses or the production of any evidence.

(2) Meetings

The Standards Board and the Board of Advisors shall each hold a meeting of its members—

(A) not less frequently than once every year for purposes of voting on the voluntary voting system guidelines referred to it under section 15362 of this title;

(B) in the case of the Standards Board, not less frequently than once every 2 years for purposes of selecting the Executive Board; and

(C) at such other times as it considers appropriate for purposes of conducting such other business as it considers appropriate consistent with this subchapter.

(b) Information from Federal Agencies

The Standards Board and the Board of Advisors may each secure directly from any Federal department or agency such information as the Board considers necessary to carry out this chapter. Upon request of the Executive Board (in the case of the Standards Board) or the Chair (in the case of the Board of Advisors), the head of such department or agency shall furnish such information to the Board.

(c) Postal Services

The Standards Board and the Board of Advisors may use the United States mails in the same manner and under the same conditions as a department or agency of the Federal Government.

(d) Administrative Support Services

Upon the request of the Executive Board (in the case of the Standards Board) or the Chair (in the case of the Board of Advisors), the Administrator of the General Services Administration shall provide to the Board, on a reimbursable basis, the administrative support services that are necessary to enable the Board to carry out its duties under this subchapter.

(e) No Compensation for Service

Members of the Standards Board and members of the Board of Advisors shall not receive any compensation for their service, but shall be paid travel expenses, including per diem in lieu of subsistence, at rates authorized for employees of agencies under subchapter I of chapter 57 of title 5, while away from their homes or regular places of business in the performance of services for the Board.

§ 15346. Status of Boards and Members for Purposes of Claims Against Board

(a) In General

The provisions of chapters 161 and 171 of title 28 shall apply with respect to the liability of the Standards Board, the Board of Advisors, and their members for acts or omissions performed pursuant to and in the course of the duties and responsibilities of the Board.

(b) Exception for Criminal Acts and Other Willful Conduct

Subsection (a) of this section may not be construed to limit personal liability for criminal acts or omissions, willful or malicious misconduct, acts or omissions for private gain, or any other act or omission outside the scope of the service of a member of the Standards Board or the Board of Advisors.

Subpart 3—Technical Guidelines Development Committee

§ 15361. Technical Guidelines Development Committee

(a) Establishment

There is hereby established the Technical Guidelines Development Committee (hereafter in this subpart referred to as the "Development Committee").

(b) Duties

(1) In General

The Development Committee shall assist the Executive Director of the Commission in the development of the voluntary voting system guidelines.

(2) Deadline for Initial Set of Recommendations

The Development Committee shall provide its first set of recommendations under this section to the Executive Director of the Commission not later than 9 months after all of its members have been appointed.

(c) Membership

(1) In General

The Development Committee shall be composed of the Director of the National Institute of Standards and Technology (who shall serve as its chair), together with a group of 14 other individuals appointed jointly by the Commission and the Director of the National Institute of Standards and Technology, consisting of the following:

 (A) An equal number of each of the following:

  (i) Members of the Standards Board.

  (ii) Members of the Board of Advisors.

  (iii) Members of the Architectural and Transportation Barrier Compliance Board under section 792 of title 29.

 (B) A representative of the American National Standards Institute.

 (C) A representative of the Institute of Electrical and Electronics Engineers.

 (D) Two representatives of the National Association of State Election Directors selected by such Association who are not members of the Standards Board or Board of Advisors, and who are not of the same political party.

 (E) Other individuals with technical and scientific expertise relating to voting systems and voting equipment.

(2) Quorum

A majority of the members of the Development Committee shall constitute a quorum, except that the Development Committee may not conduct any business prior to the appointment of all of its members.

(d) No Compensation for Service

Members of the Development Committee shall not receive any compensation for their service, but shall be paid travel expenses, including per diem in lieu of subsistence, at rates authorized for employees of agencies under subchapter I of chapter 57 of title 5, while away from their homes or regular places of business in the performance of services for the Development Committee.

(e) Technical Support from National Institute of Standards and Technology

(1) In General

At the request of the Development Committee, the Director of the National Institute of Standards and Technology shall provide the Development Committee with technical support necessary for the Development Committee to carry out its duties under this part.

(2) Technical Support

The technical support provided under paragraph (1) shall include intramural research and development in areas to support the development of the voluntary voting system guidelines under this subpart, including—

    (A) the security of computers, computer networks, and computer data storage used in voting systems, including the computerized list required under section 15483(a) of this title;

    (B) methods to detect and prevent fraud;

    (C) the protection of voter privacy;

    (D) the role of human factors in the design and application of voting systems, including assistive technologies for individuals with disabilities (including blindness) and varying levels of literacy; and

    (E) remote access voting, including voting through the Internet.

(3) No Private Sector Intellectual Property Rights in Guidelines

No private sector individual or entity shall obtain any intellectual property rights to any guideline or the contents of any guideline (or any modification to any guideline) adopted by the Commission under this chapter.

(f) Publication of Recommendations in Federal Register

At the time the Commission adopts any voluntary voting system guideline pursuant to section 15362 of this title, the Development Committee shall cause to have published in the Federal Register the recommendations it provided under this section to the Executive Director of the Commission concerning the guideline adopted.

§ 15362. Process for Adoption

(a) General requirement for notice and comment Consistent with the requirements of this section, the final adoption of the voluntary voting system guidelines (or modification of such a guideline) shall be carried out by the Commission in a manner that provides for each of the following:

    (1) Publication of notice of the proposed guidelines in the Federal Register.

    (2) An opportunity for public comment on the proposed guidelines.

(3) An opportunity for a public hearing on the record.
(4) Publication of the final guidelines in the Federal Register.

(b) Consideration of Recommendations of Development Committee; Submission of Proposed Guidelines to Board of Advisors and Standards Board

(1) Consideration of recommendations of Development Committee In developing the voluntary voting system guidelines and modifications of such guidelines under this section, the Executive Director of the Commission shall take into consideration the recommendations provided by the Technical Guidelines Development Committee under section 15361 of this title.

(2) Board of Advisors The Executive Director of the Commission shall submit the guidelines proposed to be adopted under this subpart (or any modifications to such guidelines) to the Board of Advisors.

(3) Standards Board The Executive Director of the Commission shall submit the guidelines proposed to be adopted under this subpart (or any modifications to such guidelines) to the Executive Board of the Standards Board, which shall review the guidelines (or modifications) and forward its recommendations to the Standards Board.

(c) Review

Upon receipt of voluntary voting system guidelines described in subsection (b) of this section (or a modification of such guidelines) from the Executive Director of the Commission, the Board of Advisors and the Standards Board shall each review and submit comments and recommendations regarding the guideline (or modification) to the Commission.

(d) Final Adoption

(1) In general A voluntary voting system guideline described in subsection (b) of this section (or modification of such a guideline) shall not be considered to be finally adopted by the Commission unless the Commission votes to approve the final adoption of the guideline (or modification), taking into consideration the comments and recommendations submitted by the Board of Advisors and the Standards Board under subsection (c) of this section.

The Help America Vote Act

(2) Minimum period for consideration of comments and recommendations The Commission may not vote on the final adoption of a guideline described in subsection (b) of this section (or modification of such a guideline) until the expiration of the 90-day period which begins on the date the Executive Director of the Commission submits the proposed guideline (or modification) to the Board of Advisors and the Standards Board under subsection (b) of this section.

(e) Special Rule for Initial set of Guidelines

Notwithstanding any other provision of this subpart, the most recent set of voting system standards adopted by the Federal Election Commission prior to October 29, 2002, shall be deemed to have been adopted by the Commission as of October 29, 2002, as the first set of voluntary voting system sguidelines adopted under this subpart.

Part B—Testing, Certification, Decertification, and Recertification of Voting System Hardware and Software

§ 15371. Certification and testing of voting systems

(a) Certification and Testing

(1) In general The Commission shall provide for the testing, certification, decertification, and recertification of voting system hardware and software by accredited laboratories.

(2) Optional use by States At the option of a State, the State may provide for the testing, certification, decertification, or recertification of its voting system hardware and software by the laboratories accredited by the Commission under this section.

(b) Laboratory Accreditation

(1) Recommendations by National Institute of Standards and Technology

Not later than 6 months after the Commission first adopts voluntary voting system guidelines under subpart 3 of part A of this subchapter, the Director of the National Institute of Standards and Technology shall conduct an evaluation of independent, non-Federal laboratories and shall submit to the Commission a list of those laboratories the Director proposes to be accredited to carry out the testing, certification, decertification, and recertification provided for under this section.

(2) Approval by Commission

(A) In General

The Commission shall vote on the accreditation of any laboratory under this section, taking into consideration the list submitted under paragraph (1), and no laboratory may be accredited for purposes of this section unless its accreditation is approved by a vote of the Commission.

(B) Accreditation of Laboratories Not on Director List

The Commission shall publish an explanation for the accreditation of any laboratory not included on the list submitted by the Director of the National Institute of Standards and Technology under paragraph (1).

(c) Continuing Review by National Institute of Standards and Technology

(1) In General

In cooperation with the Commission and in consultation with the Standards Board and the Board of Advisors, the Director of the National Institute of Standards and Technology shall monitor and review, on an ongoing basis, the performance of the laboratories accredited by the Commission under this section, and shall make such recommendations to the Commission as it considers appropriate with respect to the continuing accreditation of such laboratories, including recommendations to revoke the accreditation of any such laboratory.

(2) Approval by Commission Required for Revocation

The accreditation of a laboratory for purposes of this section may not be revoked unless the revocation is approved by a vote of the Commission.

(d) Transition

Until such time as the Commission provides for the testing, certification, decertification, and recertification of voting system hardware and software by accredited laboratories under this section, the accreditation of laboratories and the procedure for the testing, certification, decertification, and recertification of voting system hardware and software used as of October 29, 2002, shall remain in effect.

Part C—Studies and Other Activities to Promote Effective Administration of Federal Elections

§ 15381. Periodic Studies of Election Administration Issues

(a) In General

On such periodic basis as the Commission may determine, the Commission shall conduct and make available to the public studies regarding the election administration issues described in subsection (b) of this section, with the goal of promoting methods of voting and administering elections which—

(1) will be the most convenient, accessible, and easy to use for voters, including members of the uniformed services and overseas voters, individuals with disabilities, including the blind and visually impaired, and voters with limited proficiency in the English language;

(2) will yield the most accurate, secure, and expeditious system for voting and tabulating election results;

(3) will be nondiscriminatory and afford each registered and eligible voter an equal opportunity to vote and to have that vote counted; and

(4) will be efficient and cost-effective for use.

(b) Election Administration Issues Described

For purposes of subsection (a) of this section, the election administration issues described in this subsection are as follows:

(1) Methods and mechanisms of election technology and voting systems used in voting and counting votes in elections for Federal office, including the over-vote and under-vote notification capabilities of such technology and systems.

(2) Ballot designs for elections for Federal office.

(3) Methods of voter registration, maintaining secure and accurate lists of registered voters (including the establishment of a centralized, interactive, statewide voter registration list linked to relevant agencies and all polling sites), and ensuring that registered voters appear on the voter registration list at the appropriate polling site.

(4) Methods of conducting provisional voting.

(5) Methods of ensuring the accessibility of voting, registration, polling places, and voting equipment to all voters, including individuals with disabilities (including the blind and visually im-

paired), Native American or Alaska Native citizens, and voters with limited proficiency in the English language.

(6) Nationwide statistics and methods of identifying, deterring, and investigating voting fraud in elections for Federal office.

(7) Identifying, deterring, and investigating methods of voter intimidation.

(8) Methods of recruiting, training, and improving the performance of poll workers.

(9) Methods of educating voters about the process of registering to vote and voting, the operation of voting mechanisms, the location of polling places, and all other aspects of participating in elections.

(10) The feasibility and advisability of conducting elections for Federal office on different days, at different places, and during different hours, including the advisability of establishing a uniform poll closing time and establishing—

    (A) a legal public holiday under section 6103 of title 5 as the date on which general elections for Federal office are held;

    (B) the Tuesday next after the 1st Monday in November, in every even numbered year, as a legal public holiday under such section;

    (C) a date other than the Tuesday next after the 1st Monday in November, in every even numbered year as the date on which general elections for Federal office are held; and

    (D) any date described in subparagraph (C) as a legal public holiday under such section.

(11) Federal and State laws governing the eligibility of persons to vote.

(12) Ways that the Federal Government can best assist State and local authorities to improve the administration of elections for Federal office and what levels of funding would be necessary to provide such assistance.

(13) (A) The laws and procedures used by each State that govern—

        (i) recounts of ballots cast in elections for Federal office;

        (ii) contests of determinations regarding whether votes are counted in such elections; and

(iii) standards that define what will constitute a vote on each type of voting equipment used in the State to conduct elections for Federal office.

(B) The best practices (as identified by the Commission) that are used by States with respect to the recounts and contests described in clause (i).

(C) Whether or not there is a need for more consistency among State recount and contest procedures used with respect to elections for Federal office.

(14) The technical feasibility of providing voting materials in eight or more languages for voters who speak those languages and who have limited English proficiency.

(15) Matters particularly relevant to voting and administering elections in rural and urban areas.

(16) Methods of voter registration for members of the uniformed services and overseas voters, and methods of ensuring that such voters receive timely ballots that will be properly and expeditiously handled and counted.

(17) The best methods for establishing voting system performance benchmarks, expressed as a percentage of residual vote in the Federal contest at the top of the ballot.

(18) Broadcasting practices that may result in the broadcast of false information concerning the location or time of operation of a polling place.

(19) Such other matters as the Commission determines are appropriate.

(c) Reports

The Commission shall submit to the President and to the Committee on House Administration of the House of Representatives and the Committee on Rules and Administration of the Senate a report on each study conducted under subsection (a) of this section together with such recommendations for administrative and legislative action as the Commission determines is appropriate.

§ 15382. Study, Report, and Recommendations on Best Practices for Facilitating Military and Overseas Voting

(a) Study

(1) In General

The Commission, in consultation with the Secretary of Defense, shall conduct a study on the best practices for facilitating voting by absent uniformed services voters (as defined in section 1973ff–6(1) of this title) and overseas voters (as defined in section 1973ff–6(5) of this title).

(2) Issues Considered

In conducting the study under paragraph (1) the Commission shall consider the following issues:

(A) The rights of residence of uniformed services voters absent due to military orders.

(B) The rights of absent uniformed services voters and overseas voters to register to vote and cast absentee ballots, including the right of such voters to cast a secret ballot.

(C) The rights of absent uniformed services voters and overseas voters to submit absentee ballot applications early during an election year.

(D) The appropriate preelection deadline for mailing absentee ballots to absent uniformed services voters and overseas voters.

(E) The appropriate minimum period between the mailing of absentee ballots to absent uniformed services voters and overseas voters and the deadline for receipt of such ballots.

(F) The timely transmission of balloting materials to absent uniformed services voters and overseas voters.

(G) Security and privacy concerns in the transmission, receipt, and processing of ballots from absent uniformed services voters and overseas voters, including the need to protect against fraud.

(H) The use of a single application by absent uniformed services voters and overseas voters for absentee ballots for all Federal elections occurring during a year.

(I) The use of a single application for voter registration and absentee ballots by absent uniformed services voters and overseas voters.

(J) The use of facsimile machines and electronic means of transmission of absentee ballot applications and absentee ballots to absent uniformed services voters and overseas voters.

(K) Other issues related to the rights of absent uniformed services voters and overseas voters to participate in elections.

(b) Report and Recommendations

Not later than the date that is 18 months after October 29, 2002, the Commission shall submit to the President and Congress a report on the study conducted under subsection (a)(1) of this section together with recommendations identifying the best practices used with respect to the issues considered under subsection (a)(2) of this section.

§ 15383. Report on Human Factor Research

Not later than 1 year after October 29, 2002, the Commission, in consultation with the Director of the National Institute of Standards and Technology, shall submit a report to Congress which assesses the areas of human factor research, including usability engineering and human-computer and human-machine interaction, which feasibly could be applied to voting products and systems design to ensure the usability and accuracy of voting products and systems, including methods to improve access for individuals with disabilities (including blindness) and individuals with limited proficiency in the English language and to reduce voter error and the number of spoiled ballots in elections.

§ 15384. Study and Report on Voters Who Register by Mail and Use of Social Security Information

(a) Registration by Mail

   (1) Study

      (A) In General

      The Commission shall conduct a study of the impact of section 15483(b) of this title on voters who register by mail.

      (B) Specific Issues Studied

      The study conducted under subparagraph (A) shall include—

         (i) an examination of the impact of section 15483(b) of this title on first time mail registrant voters who vote in person, including the impact of such section on voter registration;

(ii) an examination of the impact of such section on the accuracy of voter rolls, including preventing ineligible names from being placed on voter rolls and ensuring that all eligible names are placed on voter rolls; and

(iii) an analysis of the impact of such section on existing State practices, such as the use of signature verification or attestation procedures to verify the identity of voters in elections for Federal office, and an analysis of other changes that may be made to improve the voter registration process, such as verification or additional information on the registration card.

(2) Report

Not later than 18 months after the date on which section 15483(b)(2) of this title takes effect, the Commission shall submit a report to the President and Congress on the study conducted under paragraph (1)(A) together with such recommendations for administrative and legislative action as the Commission determines is appropriate.

(b) Use of Social Security Information

Not later than 18 months after the date on which section 15483(a)(5) of this title takes effect, the Commission, in consultation with the Commissioner of Social Security, shall study and report to Congress on the feasibility and advisability of using Social Security identification numbers or other information compiled by the Social Security Administration to establish voter registration or other election law eligibility or identification requirements, including the matching of relevant information specific to an individual voter, the impact of such use on national security issues, and whether adequate safeguards or waiver procedures exist to protect the privacy of an individual voter.

§ 15385. Study and Report on Electronic Voting and the Electoral Process

(a) Study

(1) In General

The Commission shall conduct a thorough study of issues and challenges, specifically to include the potential for election fraud, presented by incorporating communications and Internet technologies in the Federal, State, and local electoral process.

(2) Issues To Be Studied

The Commission may include in the study conducted under paragraph (1) an examination of—

    (A) the appropriate security measures required and minimum standards for certification of systems or technologies in order to minimize the potential for fraud in voting or in the registration of qualified citizens to register and vote;

    (B) the possible methods, such as Internet or other communications technologies, that may be utilized in the electoral process, including the use of those technologies to register voters and enable citizens to vote online, and recommendations concerning statutes and rules to be adopted in order to implement an online or Internet system in the electoral process;

    (C) the impact that new communications or Internet technology systems for use in the electoral process could have on voter participation rates, voter education, public accessibility, potential external influences during the elections process, voter privacy and anonymity, and other issues related to the conduct and administration of elections;

    (D) whether other aspects of the electoral process, such as public availability of candidate information and citizen communication with candidates, could benefit from the increased use of online or Internet technologies;

    (E) the requirements for authorization of collection, storage, and processing of electronically generated and transmitted digital messages to permit any eligible person to register to vote or vote in an election, including applying for and casting an absentee ballot;

(F) the implementation cost of an online or Internet voting or voter registration system and the costs of elections after implementation (including a comparison of total cost savings for the administration of the electoral process by using Internet technologies or systems);

(G) identification of current and foreseeable online and Internet technologies for use in the registration of voters, for voting, or for the purpose of reducing election fraud, currently available or in use by election authorities;

(H) the means by which to ensure and achieve equity of access to online or Internet voting or voter registration systems and address the fairness of such systems to all citizens; and

(I) the impact of technology on the speed, timeliness, and accuracy of vote counts in Federal, State, and local elections.

(b) Report

(1) Submission

Not later than 20 months after October 29, 2002, the Commission shall transmit to the Committee on House Administration of the House of Representatives and the Committee on Rules and Administration of the Senate a report on the results of the study conducted under subsection (a) of this section, including such legislative recommendations or model State laws as are required to address the findings of the Commission.

(2) Internet Posting

In addition to the dissemination requirements under chapter 19 of title 44, the Election Administration Commission shall post the report transmitted under paragraph (1) on an Internet website.

§ 15386. Study and Report on Free Absentee Ballot Postage

(a) Study on the Establishment of a Free Absentee Ballot Postage Program

(1) In General

The Commission, in consultation with the Postal Service, shall conduct a study on the feasibility and advisability of the establishment of a program under which the Postal Service shall waive or otherwise reduce the amount of postage applicable with respect to absentee ballots submitted by voters in general elections for Federal office (other than balloting materials mailed under section 3406 of title 39) that does not apply with respect to the postage required to send the absentee ballots to voters.

(2) Public Survey

As part of the study conducted under paragraph (1), the Commission shall conduct a survey of potential beneficiaries under the program described in such paragraph, including the elderly and disabled, and shall take into account the results of such survey in determining the feasibility and advisability of establishing such a program.

(b) Report

(1) Submission

Not later than the date that is 1 year after October 29, 2002, the Commission shall submit to Congress a report on the study conducted under subsection (a)(1) of this section together with recommendations for such legislative and administrative action as the Commission determines appropriate.

(2) Costs

The report submitted under paragraph (1) shall contain an estimate of the costs of establishing the program described in subsection (a)(1) of this section.

(3) Implementation

The report submitted under paragraph (1) shall contain an analysis of the feasibility of implementing the program described in subsection (a)(1) of this section with respect to the absentee ballots to be submitted in the general election for Federal office held in 2004.

(4) Recommendations Regarding the Elderly and Disabled

The report submitted under paragraph (1) shall—

(A) include recommendations on ways that program described in subsection (a)(1) of this section would target elderly individuals and individuals with disabilities; and

(B) identify methods to increase the number of such individuals who vote in elections for Federal office.

(c) Postal Service Defined

The term "Postal Service" means the United States Postal Service established under section 201 of title 39.

§ 15387. Consultation with Standards Board and Board of Advisors

The Commission shall carry out its duties under this part in consultation with the Standards Board and the Board of Advisors.

Part D—Election Assistance

Subpart 1—Requirements Payments

§ 15401. Requirements Payments

(a) In General

The Commission shall make a requirements payment each year in an amount determined under section 15402 of this title to each State which meets the conditions described in section 15403 of this title for the year.

(b) Use of Funds

   (1) In General

   Except as provided in paragraphs (2) and (3), a State receiving a requirements payment shall use the payment only to meet the requirements of subchapter III of this chapter.

   (2) Other Activities

   A State may use a requirements payment to carry out other activities to improve the administration of elections for Federal office if the State certifies to the Commission that—

      (A) the State has implemented the requirements of subchapter III of this chapter; or

      (B) the amount expended with respect to such other activities does not exceed an amount equal to the minimum payment amount applicable to the State under section 15402(c) of this title.

(3) Activities Under Uniformed and Overseas Citizens Absentee Voting Act[214]

A State shall use a requirements payment made using funds appropriated pursuant to the authorization under section 15407(a)(4) of this title only to meet the requirements under the Uniformed and Overseas Citizens Absentee Voting Act [42 U.S.C. 1973ff et seq.] imposed as a result of the provisions of and amendments made by the Military and Overseas Voter Empowerment Act.

(c) Retroactive Payments

(1) In General

Notwithstanding any other provision of this part, including the maintenance of effort requirements of section 15404(a)(7) of this title, a State may use a requirements payment as a reimbursement for costs incurred in obtaining voting equipment which meets the requirements of section 15481 of this title if the State obtains the equipment after the regularly scheduled general election for Federal office held in November 2000.

(2) Special Rule Regarding Multiyear Contracts

A State may use a requirements payment for any costs for voting equipment which meets the requirements of section 15481 of this title that, pursuant to a multiyear contract, were incurred on or after January 1, 2001, except that the amount that the State is otherwise required to contribute under the maintenance of effort requirements of section 15404(a)(7) of this title shall be increased by the amount of the payment made with respect to such multiyear contract.

(d) Adoption of Commission Guidelines and Guidance Not Required to Receive Payment

Nothing in this subpart may be construed to require a State to implement any of the voluntary voting system guidelines or any of the voluntary guidance adopted by the Commission with respect to any matter as a condition for receiving a requirements payment.

---

214. Subsection added by National Defense Authorization Act for Fiscal Year 2010, Pub. L. 111-84, 123 Stat. 2189, 2333 (2009).

(e) Schedule of Payments

As soon as practicable after the initial appointment of all members of the Commission (but in no event later than 6 months thereafter), and not less frequently than once each calendar year thereafter, the Commission shall make requirements payments to States under this subpart.

(f) Limitation

A State may not use any portion of a requirements payment—
    (1) to pay costs associated with any litigation, except to the extent that such costs otherwise constitute permitted uses of a requirements payment under this subpart; or
    (2) for the payment of any judgment.

§ 15402. Allocation of Funds

(a) In General

Subject to subsection (c) of this section, the amount of a requirements payment made to a State for a year shall be equal to the product of—
    (1) the total amount appropriated for requirements payments for the year pursuant to the authorization under section 15407 of this title; and
    (2) the State allocation percentage for the State (as determined under subsection (b) of this section).

(b) State Allocation Percentage Defined

The "State allocation percentage" for a State is the amount (expressed as a percentage) equal to the quotient of—
    (1) the voting age population of the State (as reported in the most recent decennial census); and
    (2) the total voting age population of all States (as reported in the most recent decennial census).

(c) Minimum Amount of Payment

The amount of a requirements payment made to a State for a year may not be less than—
    (1) in the case of any of the several States or the District of Columbia, one-half of 1 percent of the total amount appropriated for requirements payments for the year under section 15407 of this title; or

(2) in the case of the Commonwealth of Puerto Rico, Guam, American Samoa, or the United States Virgin Islands, one-tenth of 1 percent of such total amount.

(d) Pro Rata Reductions

The Administrator shall make such pro rata reductions to the allocations determined under subsection (a) of this section as are necessary to comply with the requirements of subsection (c) of this section.

(e) Continuing Availability of Funds After Appropriation

A requirements payment made to a State under this subpart shall be available to the State without fiscal year limitation.

§ 15403. Condition for Receipt of Funds

(a) In General

A State is eligible to receive a requirements payment for a fiscal year if the chief executive officer of the State, or designee, in consultation and coordination with the chief State election official, has filed with the Commission a statement certifying that the State is in compliance with the requirements referred to in subsection (b) of this section. A State may meet the requirement of the previous sentence by filing with the Commission a statement which reads as follows: "_____ hereby certifies that it is in compliance with the requirements referred to in section 253(b) of the Help America Vote Act of 2002." (with the blank to be filled in with the name of the State involved).

(b) State Plan Requirement; Certification of Compliance with Applicable Laws and Requirements

The requirements referred to in this subsection are as follows:

(1) The State has filed with the Commission a State plan covering the fiscal year which the State certifies—

(A) contains each of the elements described in section 15404(a) of this title (or, for purposes of determining the eligibility of a State to receive a requirements payment appropriated pursuant to the authorization provided under section 15407(a)(4) of this title, contains the element described in paragraph (14) of such section) with respect to the fiscal year;[215]

(B) is developed in accordance with section 15405 of this title; and

(C) meets the public notice and comment requirements of section 15406 of this title.

(2) (A) Subject to subparagraph (B), the State has filed with the Commission a plan for the implementation of the uniform, nondiscriminatory administrative complaint procedures required under section 15512 of this title (or has included such a plan in the State plan filed under paragraph (1)), and has such procedures in place for purposes of meeting the requirements of such section. If the State does not include such an implementation plan in the State plan filed under paragraph (1), the requirements of sections 15405(b) and 15406 of this title shall apply to the implementation plan in the same manner as such requirements apply to the State plan.

(B)[216] Subparagraph (A) shall not apply for purposes of determining the eligibility of a State to receive a requirements payment appropriated pursuant to the authorization provided under section 15407(a)(4) of this title.

(3) The State is in compliance with each of the laws described in section 15545 of this title, as such laws apply with respect to this chapter.

(4) To the extent that any portion of the requirements payment is used for activities other than meeting the requirements of subchapter III of this chapter—

(A) the State's proposed uses of the requirements payment are not inconsistent with the requirements of subchapter III of this chapter; and

---

215. The National Defense Authorization Act for Fiscal Year 2010, *id.*, substituted "section 15404(a) of this title (or, for purposes of determining the eligibility of a State to receive a requirements payment appropriated pursuant to the authorization provided under section 15407(a)(4) of this title, contains the element described in paragraph (14) of such section)" for "section 15404 of this title."

216. Subparagraph added by the National Defense Authorization Act for Fiscal Year 2010, *id.*

(B) the use of the funds under this paragraph is consistent with the requirements of section 15401(b) of this title.

(5) (A) Subject to subparagraph (B), the State has appropriated funds for carrying out the activities for which the requirements payment is made in an amount equal to 5 percent of the total amount to be spent for such activities (taking into account the requirements payment and the amount spent by the State) and, in the case of a State that uses a requirements payment as a reimbursement under section 15401(c)(2) of this title, an additional amount equal to the amount of such reimbursement.

(B)[217] Subparagraph (A) shall not apply for purposes of determining the eligibility of a State to receive a requirements payment appropriated pursuant to the authorization provided under section 15407(a)(4) of this title for fiscal year 2010, except that if the State does not appropriate funds in accordance with subparagraph (A) prior to the last day of fiscal year 2011, the State shall repay to the Commission the requirements payment which is appropriated pursuant to such authorization.

(c) Methods of Compliance Left to Discretion of State

The specific choices on the methods of complying with the elements of a State plan shall be left to the discretion of the State.

(d) Timing for Filing of Certification

A State may not file a statement of certification under subsection (a) of this section until the expiration of the 45-day period (or, in the case of a fiscal year other than the first fiscal year for which a requirements payment is made to the State under this part, the 30-day period) which begins on the date notice of[218] the State plan under this part is published in the Federal Register pursuant to section 15405(b) of this title.

---

217. Subparagraph added by the National Defense Authorization Act for Fiscal Year 2010, *id.*, 123 Stat. at 2333–34.

218. The phrase "notice of" was added by the Consolidated Appropriations Act for Fiscal Year 2012, Pub. L. 112-74, 125 Stat. 785, 927 (2011).

(e) Chief State Election Official Defined

In this part, the "chief State election official" of a State is the individual designated by the State under section 10 of the National Voter Registration Act of 1993 (42 U.S.C. 1973gg–8) to be responsible for coordination of the State's responsibilities under such Act.

§ 15404. State Plan

(a) In General

The State plan shall contain a description of each of the following:

(1) How the State will use the requirements payment to meet the requirements of subchapter III of this chapter, and, if applicable under section 15401(a)(2) of this title, to carry out other activities to improve the administration of elections.

(2) How the State will distribute and monitor the distribution of the requirements payment to units of local government or other entities in the State for carrying out the activities described in paragraph (1), including a description of—

(A) the criteria to be used to determine the eligibility of such units or entities for receiving the payment; and

(B) the methods to be used by the State to monitor the performance of the units or entities to whom the payment is distributed, consistent with the performance goals and measures adopted under paragraph (8).

(3) How the State will provide for programs for voter education, election official education and training, and poll worker training which will assist the State in meeting the requirements of subchapter III of this chapter.

(4) How the State will adopt voting system guidelines and processes which are consistent with the requirements of section 15481 of this title.

(5) How the State will establish a fund described in subsection (b) of this section for purposes of administering the State's activities under this subpart, including information on fund management.

(6) The State's proposed budget for activities under this subpart, based on the State's best estimates of the costs of such activities and the amount of funds to be made available, including specific information on—

(A) the costs of the activities required to be carried out to meet the requirements of subchapter III of this chapter;

(B) the portion of the requirements payment which will be used to carry out activities to meet such requirements; and

(C) the portion of the requirements payment which will be used to carry out other activities.

(7) How the State, in using the requirements payment, will maintain the expenditures of the State for activities funded by the payment at a level that is not less than the level of such expenditures maintained by the State for the fiscal year ending prior to November 2000.

(8) How the State will adopt performance goals and measures that will be used by the State to determine its success and the success of units of local government in the State in carrying out the plan, including timetables for meeting each of the elements of the plan, descriptions of the criteria the State will use to measure performance and the process used to develop such criteria, and a description of which official is to be held responsible for ensuring that each performance goal is met.

(9) A description of the uniform, nondiscriminatory State-based administrative complaint procedures in effect under section 15512 of this title.

(10) If the State received any payment under subchapter I of this chapter, a description of how such payment will affect the activities proposed to be carried out under the plan, including the amount of funds available for such activities.

(11) How the State will conduct ongoing management of the plan, except that the State may not make any material change in the administration of the plan unless notice of[219] the change—

(A) is developed and published in the Federal Register in accordance with section 15405 of this title in the same manner as the State plan;

(B) is subject to public notice and comment in accordance with section 15406 of this title in the same manner as the State plan; and

---

219. The phrase "notice of" was added by the Consolidated Appropriations Act of 2012, *id.*

(C) takes effect only after the expiration of the 30-day period which begins on the date notice of[220] the change is published in the Federal Register in accordance with subparagraph (A).

(12) In the case of a State with a State plan in effect under this part during the previous fiscal year, a description of how the plan reflects changes from the State plan for the previous fiscal year and of how the State succeeded in carrying out the State plan for such previous fiscal year.

(13) A description of the committee which participated in the development of the State plan in accordance with section 15405 of this title and the procedures followed by the committee under such section and section 15406 of this title.

(14)[221] How the State will comply with the provisions and requirements of and amendments made by the Military and Overseas Voter Empowerment Act.

(b) Requirements for Election Fund

(1) Election fund described For purposes of subsection (a)(5) of this section, a fund described in this subsection with respect to a State is a fund which is established in the treasury of the State government, which is used in accordance with paragraph (2), and which consists of the following amounts:

(A) Amounts appropriated or otherwise made available by the State for carrying out the activities for which the requirements payment is made to the State under this subpart.

(B) The requirements payment made to the State under this subpart.

(C) Such other amounts as may be appropriated under law.

(D) Interest earned on deposits of the fund.

---

220. The phrase "notice of" was added by the Consolidated Appropriations Act of 2012, *id.*

221. Paragraph added by the National Defense Authorization Act for Fiscal Year 2010, Pub. L. 111-84, 123 Stat. 2189, 2333 (2009).

(2) Use of Fund

Amounts in the fund shall be used by the State exclusively to carry out the activities for which the requirements payment is made to the State under this subpart.

(3) Treatment of States That Require Changes to State Law

In the case of a State that requires State legislation to establish the fund described in this subsection, the Commission shall defer disbursement of the requirements payment to such State until such time as legislation establishing the fund is enacted.

(c) Protection Against Actions Based on Information in Plan

(1) In General

No action may be brought under this chapter against a State or other jurisdiction on the basis of any information contained in the State plan filed under this subpart.

(2) Exception for Criminal Acts

Paragraph (1) may not be construed to limit the liability of a State or other jurisdiction for criminal acts or omissions.

§ 15405. Process for Development and Filing of Plan; Publication by Commission

(a) In General

The chief State election official shall develop the State plan under this part through a committee of appropriate individuals, including the chief election officials of the two most populous jurisdictions within the States, other local election officials, stake holders (including representatives of groups of individuals with disabilities), and other citizens, appointed for such purpose by the chief State election official.

(b) Publication of Plan by Commission

After receiving the State plan of a State under this part, the Commission shall cause to have the plan posted on the Commission's website with a notice published in the Federal Register.[222]

---

222. The Consolidated Appropriations Act for Fiscal Year 2012, Pub. L. 112-74, 125 Stat. 785, 926 (2011), inserted "posted on the Commission's website with a notice" after "cause to have the plan."

§ 15406. Requirement for Public Notice and Comment

For purposes of section 15401(a)(1)(C) of this title, a State plan meets the public notice and comment requirements of this section if—

>(1) not later than 30 days prior to the submission of the plan, the State made a preliminary version of the plan available for public inspection and comment;

>(2) the State publishes notice that the preliminary version of the plan is so available; and

>(3) the State took the public comments made regarding the preliminary version of the plan into account in preparing the plan which was filed with the Commission.

§ 15407. Authorization of Appropriations

(a) In General

In addition to amounts transferred under section 15304(c) of this title, there are authorized to be appropriated for requirements payments under this subpart the following amounts:

>(1) For fiscal year 2003, $1,400,000,000.

>(2) For fiscal year 2004, $1,000,000,000.

>(3) For fiscal year 2005, $600,000,000.

>(4)[223] For fiscal year 2010 and subsequent fiscal years, such sums as are necessary for purposes of making requirements payments to States to carry out the activities described in section 15401(b)(3) of this title.

(b) Availability

Any amounts appropriated pursuant to the authority of subsection (a) of this section shall remain available without fiscal year limitation until expended.

§ 15408. Reports

Not later than 6 months after the end of each fiscal year for which a State received a requirements payment under this subpart, the State shall submit a report to the Commission on the activities conducted with the funds provided during the year, and shall include in the report—

---

223. Paragraph added by the National Defense Authorization Act for Fiscal Year 2010, Pub. L. 111-84, 123 Stat. 2189, 233f (2009).

(1) a list of expenditures made with respect to each category of activities described in section 15401(b) of this title;

(2) the number and type of articles of voting equipment obtained with the funds; and

(3) an analysis and description of the activities funded under this subpart to meet the requirements of this chapter and an analysis and description of how such activities conform to the State plan under section 15404 of this title.

Subpart 2—Payments to States and Units of Local Government to Assure Access for Individuals with Disabilities

§ 15421. Payments to States and Units of Local Government to Assure Access for Individuals with Disabilities

(a) In General

The Secretary of Health and Human Services shall make a payment to each eligible State and each eligible unit of local government (as described in section 15423 of this title).

(b) Use of Funds

An eligible State and eligible unit of local government shall use the payment received under this subpart for—

(1) making polling places, including the path of travel, entrances, exits, and voting areas of each polling facility, accessible to individuals with disabilities, including the blind and visually impaired, in a manner that provides the same opportunity for access and participation (including privacy and independence) as for other voters; and

(2) providing individuals with disabilities and the other individuals described in paragraph (1) with information about the accessibility of polling places, including outreach programs to inform the individuals about the availability of accessible polling places and training election officials, poll workers, and election volunteers on how best to promote the access and participation of individuals with disabilities in elections for Federal office.

(c) Schedule of Payments

As soon as practicable after October 29, 2002 (but in no event later than 6 months thereafter), and not less frequently than once each calendar year thereafter, the Secretary shall make payments under this subpart.

§ 15422. Amount of Payment

(a) In General

The amount of a payment made to an eligible State or an eligible unit of local government for a year under this subpart shall be determined by the Secretary.

(b) Continuing Availability of Funds After Appropriation

A payment made to an eligible State or eligible unit of local government under this subpart shall be available without fiscal year limitation.

§ 15423. Requirements for Eligibility

(a) Application

Each State or unit of local government that desires to receive a payment under this subpart for a fiscal year shall submit an application for the payment to the Secretary at such time and in such manner and containing such information as the Secretary shall require.

(b) Contents of Application

Each application submitted under subsection (a) of this section shall—

(1) describe the activities for which assistance under this section is sought; and

(2) provide such additional information and certifications as the Secretary determines to be essential to ensure compliance with the requirements of this subpart.

(c) Protection Against Actions Based on Information in Application

(1) In General

No action may be brought under this chapter against a State or unit of local government on the basis of any information contained in the application submitted under subsection (a) of this section.

(2) Exception for Criminal Acts

Paragraph (1) may not be construed to limit the liability of a State or unit of local government for criminal acts or omissions.

§ 15424. Authorization of Appropriations

(a) In General

There are authorized to be appropriated to carry out the provisions of this subpart the following amounts:
    (1) For fiscal year 2003, $50,000,000.
    (2) For fiscal year 2004, $25,000,000.
    (3) For fiscal year 2005, $25,000,000.

(b) Availability

Any amounts appropriated pursuant to the authority of subsection (a) of this section shall remain available without fiscal year limitation until expended.

§ 15425. Reports

(a) Reports by Recipients

Not later than the 6 months after the end of each fiscal year for which an eligible State or eligible unit of local government received a payment under this subpart, the State or unit shall submit a report to the Secretary on the activities conducted with the funds provided during the year, and shall include in the report a list of expenditures made with respect to each category of activities described in section 15421(b) of this title.

(b) Report by Secretary to Committees

With respect to each fiscal year for which the Secretary makes payments under this subpart, the Secretary shall submit a report on the activities carried out under this subpart to the Committee on House Administration of the House of Representatives and the Committee on Rules and Administration of the Senate.

Subpart 3—Grants for Research on Voting Technology Improvements

§ 15441. Grants for Research on Voting Technology Improvements

(a) In General

The Commission shall make grants to assist entities in carrying out research and development to improve the quality, reliability, accuracy, accessibility, affordability, and security of voting equipment, election systems, and voting technology.

(b) Eligibility

An entity is eligible to receive a grant under this subpart if it submits to the Commission (at such time and in such form as the Commission may require) an application containing—

(1) certifications that the research and development funded with the grant will take into account the need to make voting equipment fully accessible for individuals with disabilities, including the blind and visually impaired, the need to ensure that such individuals can vote independently and with privacy, and the need to provide alternative language accessibility for individuals with limited proficiency in the English language (consistent with the requirements of the Voting Rights Act of 1965 [42 U.S.C. 1973 et seq.]); and

(2) such other information and certifications as the Commission may require.

(c) Applicability of Regulations Governing Patent Rights in Inventions Made with Federal Assistance

Any invention made by the recipient of a grant under this subpart using funds provided under this subpart shall be subject to chapter 18 of title 35 (relating to patent rights in inventions made with Federal assistance).

(d) Recommendation of topics for research

(1) In General

The Director of the National Institute of Standards and Technology (hereafter in this section referred to as the "Director") shall submit to the Commission an annual list of the Director's suggestions for issues which may be the subject of research funded with grants awarded under this subpart during the year.

(2) Review of Grant Applications Received by Commission

The Commission shall submit each application it receives for a grant under this subpart to the Director, who shall review the application and provide the Commission with such comments as the Director considers appropriate.

(3) Monitoring and Adjustment of Grant Activities at Request of Commission

After the Commission has awarded a grant under this subpart, the Commission may request that the Director monitor the grant, and (to the extent permitted under the terms of the grant as awarded) the Director may recommend to the Commission that the recipient of the grant modify and adjust the activities carried out under the grant.

(4) Evaluation of Grants at Request of Commission

(A) In General

In the case of a grant for which the Commission submits the application to the Director under paragraph (2) or requests that the Director monitor the grant under paragraph (3), the Director shall prepare and submit to the Commission an evaluation of the grant and the activities carried out under the grant.

(B) Inclusion in Reports

The Commission shall include the evaluations submitted under subparagraph (A) for a year in the report submitted for the year under section 15327 of this title. (e) Provision of information on projects The Commission may provide to the Technical Guidelines Development Committee under subpart 3 of part A of this subchapter such information regarding the activities funded under this subpart as the Commission deems necessary to assist the Committee in carrying out its duties.

§ 15442. Report

(a) In General

Each entity which receives a grant under this subpart shall submit to the Commission a report describing the activities carried out with the funds provided under the grant.

(b) Deadline

An entity shall submit a report required under subsection (a) of this section not later than 60 days after the end of the fiscal year for which the entity received the grant which is the subject of the report.

§ 15443. Authorization of Appropriations

(a) In General

There are authorized to be appropriated for grants under this subpart $20,000,000 for fiscal year 2003.

(b) Availability of Funds

Amounts appropriated pursuant to the authorization under this section shall remain available, without fiscal year limitation, until expended.

Subpart 4—Pilot Program for Testing of Equipment and Technology

§ 15451. Pilot program

(a) In General

The Commission shall make grants to carry out pilot programs under which new technologies in voting systems and equipment are tested and implemented on a trial basis so that the results of such tests and trials are reported to Congress.

(b) Eligibility

An entity is eligible to receive a grant under this subpart if it submits to the Commission (at such time and in such form as the Commission may require) an application containing—

    (1) certifications that the pilot programs funded with the grant will take into account the need to make voting equipment fully accessible for individuals with disabilities, including the blind and visually impaired, the need to ensure that such individuals can vote independently and with privacy, and the need to provide alternative language accessibility for individuals with limited proficiency in the English language (consistent with the requirements of the Voting Rights Act of 1965 [42 U.S.C. 1973 et seq.] and the requirements of this chapter); and

    (2) such other information and certifications as the Commission may require.

(c) Recommendation of Topics for Pilot Programs

    (1) In General

The Director of the National Institute of Standards and Technology (hereafter in this section referred to as the "Director") shall submit to the Commission an annual list of the Director's suggestions for issues which may be the subject of pilot programs funded with grants awarded under this subpart during the year.

(2) Review of Grant Applications Received by Commission

The Commission shall submit each application it receives for a grant under this subpart to the Director, who shall review the application and provide the Commission with such comments as the Director considers appropriate.

(3) Monitoring and Adjustment of Grant Activities at Request of Commission

After the Commission has awarded a grant under this subpart, the Commission may request that the Director monitor the grant, and (to the extent permitted under the terms of the grant as awarded) the Director may recommend to the Commission that the recipient of the grant modify and adjust the activities carried out under the grant.

(4) Evaluation of Grants at Request of Commission

(A) In General

In the case of a grant for which the Commission submits the application to the Director under paragraph (2) or requests that the Director monitor the grant under paragraph (3), the Director shall prepare and submit to the Commission an evaluation of the grant and the activities carried out under the grant.

(B) Inclusion in Reports

The Commission shall include the evaluations submitted under subparagraph (A) for a year in the report submitted for the year under section 15327 of this title.

(d) Provision of Information on Projects

The Commission may provide to the Technical Guidelines Development Committee under subpart 3 of part A of this subchapter such information regarding the activities funded under this subpart as the Commission deems necessary to assist the Committee in carrying out its duties.

§ 15452. Report

(a) In General

Each entity which receives a grant under this subpart shall submit to the Commission a report describing the activities carried out with the funds provided under the grant.

(b) Deadline

An entity shall submit a report required under subsection (a) of this section not later than 60 days after the end of the fiscal year for which the entity received the grant which is the subject of the report.

§ 15453. Authorization of Appropriations

(a) In General

There are authorized to be appropriated for grants under this subpart $10,000,000 for fiscal year 2003.

(b) Availability of Funds

Amounts appropriated pursuant to the authorization under this section shall remain available, without fiscal year limitation, until expended.

Subpart 5—Protection and Advocacy Systems

§ 15461. Payments for Protection and Advocacy Systems

(a) In General

In addition to any other payments made under this part, the Secretary of Health and Human Services shall pay the protection and advocacy system (as defined in section 102 of the Developmental Disabilities Assistance and Bill of Rights Act of 2000 (42 U.S.C. 15002)) of each State to ensure full participation in the electoral process for individuals with disabilities, including registering to vote, casting a vote and accessing polling places. In providing such services, protection and advocacy systems shall have the same general authorities as they are afforded under subtitle C of title I of the Developmental Disabilities Assistance and Bill of Rights Act of 2000 (42 U.S.C. 15041 et seq.).

(b) Minimum Grant Amount

The minimum amount of each grant to a protection and advocacy system shall be determined and allocated as set forth in subsections (c)(3), (c)(4), (c)(5), (e), and (g) of section 794e of title 29, except that the amount of the grants to systems referred to in subsections (c)(3)(B) and (c)(4)(B) of that section shall be not less than $70,000 and $35,000, respectively.

(c) Training and Technical Assistance Program

(1) In General

Not later than 90 days after the date on which the initial appropriation of funds for a fiscal year is made pursuant to the authorization under section 15462 of this title, the Secretary shall set aside 7 percent of the amount appropriated under such section and use such portion to make payments to eligible entities to provide training and technical assistance with respect to the activities carried out under this section.

(2) Use of Funds

A recipient of a payment under this subsection may use the payment to support training in the use of voting systems and technologies, and to demonstrate and evaluate the use of such systems and technologies, by individuals with disabilities (including blindness) in order to assess the availability and use of such systems and technologies for such individuals. At least one of the recipients under this subsection shall use the payment to provide training and technical assistance for nonvisual access.

(3) Eligibility

An entity is eligible to receive a payment under this subsection if the entity—

    (A) is a public or private nonprofit entity with demonstrated experience in voting issues for individuals with disabilities;

    (B) is governed by a board with respect to

which the majority of its members are individuals with disabilities or family members of such individuals or individuals who are blind; and

    (C) submits to the Secretary an application at such time, in such manner, and containing such information as the Secretary may require.

§ 15462. Authorization of Appropriations

(a) In General

In addition to any other amounts authorized to be appropriated under this part, there are authorized to be appropriated $10,000,000 for each of the fiscal years 2003, 2004, 2005, and 2006, and for each subsequent fiscal year such sums as may be necessary, for the purpose of making payments under section 15461(a) of this title; except that none of the funds provided by this subsection shall be used to initiate or otherwise participate in any litigation related to election-related disability access, notwithstanding the general authorities that the protection and advocacy systems are otherwise afforded under subtitle C of title I of the Developmental Disabilities Assistance and Bill of Rights Act of 2000 (42 U.S.C. 15041 et seq.).

(b) Availability

Any amounts appropriated pursuant to the authority of this section shall remain available until expended.

Subpart 6—National Student and Parent Mock Election
§ 15471. National Student and Parent Mock Election

(a) In General

The Election Assistance Commission is authorized to award grants to the National Student and Parent Mock Election, a national nonprofit, nonpartisan organization that works to promote voter participation in American elections to enable it to carry out voter education activities for students and their parents. Such activities may—

(1) include simulated national elections at least 5 days before the actual election that permit participation by students and parents from each of the 50 States in the United States, its territories, the District of Columbia, and United States schools overseas; and

(2) consist of—

(A) school forums and local cable call-in shows on the national issues to be voted upon in an "issues forum";

(B) speeches and debates before students and parents by local candidates or stand-ins for such candidates;

(C) quiz team competitions, mock press conferences, and speech writing competitions;

(D) weekly meetings to follow the course of the campaign; or

(E) school and neighborhood campaigns to increase voter turnout, including newsletters, posters, telephone chains, and transportation.

(b) Requirement

The National Student and Parent Mock Election shall present awards to outstanding student and parent mock election projects.

§ 15472. Authorization of Appropriations

There are authorized to be appropriated to carry out the provisions of this part $200,000 for fiscal year 2003 and such sums as may be necessary for each of the 6 succeeding fiscal years.

Subchapter III—Uniform and Nondiscriminatory Election Technology and Administration Requirements[224]

Part A—Requirements

§ 15481. Voting Systems Standards[225]

(a) Requirements

Each voting system used in an election for Federal office shall meet the following requirements:

(1) In General

(A) Except as provided in subparagraph (B), the voting system (including any lever voting system, optical scanning voting system, or direct recording electronic system) shall—

(i) permit the voter to verify (in a private and independent manner) the votes selected by the voter on the ballot before the ballot is cast and counted;

(ii) provide the voter with the opportunity (in a private and independent manner) to change the ballot or correct any error before the ballot is cast and counted (including the opportunity to correct the error through the issuance of a replacement ballot if the voter was otherwise unable to change the ballot or correct any error); and

(iii) if the voter selects votes for more than one candidate for a single office—

---

224. Title III.
225. Section 301.

The Help America Vote Act

        (I) notify the voter that the voter has selected more than one candidate for a single office on the ballot;

        (II) notify the voter before the ballot is cast and counted of the effect of casting multiple votes for the office; and

        (III) provide the voter with the opportunity to correct the ballot before the ballot is cast and counted.

  (B) A State or jurisdiction that uses a paper ballot voting system, a punch card voting system, or a central count voting system (including mail-in absentee ballots and mail-in ballots), may meet the requirements of subparagraph (A)(iii) by—

        (i) establishing a voter education program specific to that voting system that notifies each voter of the effect of casting multiple votes for an office; and

        (ii) providing the voter with instructions on how to correct the ballot before it is cast and counted (including instructions on how to correct the error through the issuance of a replacement ballot if the voter was otherwise unable to change the ballot or correct any error).

  (C) The voting system shall ensure that any notification required under this paragraph preserves the privacy of the voter and the confidentiality of the ballot.

(2) Audit Capacity

(A) In General

The voting system shall produce a record with an audit capacity for such system.

(B) Manual Audit Capacity

        (i) The voting system shall produce a permanent paper record with a manual audit capacity for such system.

        (ii) The voting system shall provide the voter with an opportunity to change the ballot or correct any error before the permanent paper record is produced.

        (iii) The paper record produced under subparagraph (A) shall be available as an official record for any recount conducted with respect to any election in which the system is used.

(3) Accessibility for Individuals with Disabilities

The voting system shall—

(A) be accessible for individuals with disabilities, including nonvisual accessibility for the blind and visually impaired, in a manner that provides the same opportunity for access and participation (including privacy and independence) as for other voters;

(B) satisfy the requirement of subparagraph (A) through the use of at least one direct recording electronic voting system or other voting system equipped for individuals with disabilities at each polling place; and

(C) if purchased with funds made available under subchapter II of this chapter on or after January 1, 2007, meet the voting system standards for disability access (as outlined in this paragraph).

(4) Alternative Language Accessibility

The voting system shall provide alternative language accessibility pursuant to the requirements of section 1973aa–1a of this title.

(5) Error Rates

The error rate of the voting system in counting ballots (determined by taking into account only those errors which are attributable to the voting system and not attributable to an act of the voter) shall comply with the error rate standards established under section 3.2.1 of the voting systems standards issued by the Federal Election Commission which are in effect on October 29, 2002.

(6) Uniform Definition of What Constitutes a Vote

Each State shall adopt uniform and nondiscriminatory standards that define what constitutes a vote and what will be counted as a vote for each category of voting system used in the State.

(b) Voting System Defined

In this section, the term "voting system" means—

(1) the total combination of mechanical, electromechanical, or electronic equipment (including the software, firmware, and

documentation required to program, control, and support the equipment) that is used—
  (A) to define ballots;
  (B) to cast and count votes;
  (C) to report or display election results; and
  (D) to maintain and produce any audit trail information; and
(2) the practices and associated documentation used—
  (A) to identify system components and versions of such components;
  (B) to test the system during its development and maintenance;
  (C) to maintain records of system errors and defects;
  (D) to determine specific system changes to be made to a system after the initial qualification of the system; and
  (E) to make available any materials to the voter (such as notices, instructions, forms, or paper ballots).

(c) Construction

  (1) In general Nothing in this section shall be construed to prohibit a State or jurisdiction which used a particular type of voting system in the elections for Federal office held in November 2000 from using the same type of system after the effective date of this section, so long as the system meets or is modified to meet the requirements of this section.
  (2) Protection of paper ballot voting systems For purposes of subsection (a)(1)(A)(i) of this section, the term "verify" may not be defined in a manner that makes it impossible for a paper ballot voting system to meet the requirements of such subsection or to be modified to meet such requirements.

(d) Effective Date

Each State and jurisdiction shall be required to comply with the requirements of this section on and after January 1, 2006.

§ 15482. Provisional Voting and Voting Information Requirements[226]

(a) Provisional Voting Requirements

If an individual declares that such individual is a registered voter in the jurisdiction in which the individual desires to vote and that the individual is eligible to vote in an election for Federal office, but the name of the individual does not appear on the official list of eligible voters for the polling place or an election official asserts that the individual is not eligible to vote, such individual shall be permitted to cast a provisional ballot as follows:

(1) An election official at the polling place shall notify the individual that the individual may cast a provisional ballot in that election.

(2) The individual shall be permitted to cast a provisional ballot at that polling place upon the execution of a written affirmation by the individual before an election official at the polling place stating that the individual is—

(A) a registered voter in the jurisdiction in which the individual desires to vote; and

(B) eligible to vote in that election.

(3) An election official at the polling place shall transmit the ballot cast by the individual or the voter information contained in the written affirmation executed by the individual under paragraph (2) to an appropriate State or local election official for prompt verification under paragraph (4).

(4) If the appropriate State or local election official to whom the ballot or voter information is transmitted under paragraph (3) determines that the individual is eligible under State law to vote, the individual's provisional ballot shall be counted as a vote in that election in accordance with State law.

(5) (A) At the time that an individual casts a provisional ballot, the appropriate State or local election official shall give the individual written information that states that any individual who casts a provisional ballot will be able to ascertain under the system established under subparagraph (B) whether the vote was counted, and, if the vote was not counted, the reason that the vote was not counted.

---

226. Section 302.

(B) The appropriate State or local election official shall establish a free access system (such as a toll-free telephone number or an Internet website) that any individual who casts a provisional ballot may access to discover whether the vote of that individual was counted, and, if the vote was not counted, the reason that the vote was not counted. States described in section 1973gg–2(b) of this title may meet the requirements of this subsection using voter registration procedures established under applicable State law. The appropriate State or local official shall establish and maintain reasonable procedures necessary to protect the security, confidentiality, and integrity of personal information collected, stored, or otherwise used by the free access system established under paragraph (5)(B). Access to information about an individual provisional ballot shall be restricted to the individual who cast the ballot.

(b) Voting Information Requirements

(1) Public Posting on Election Day

The appropriate State or local election official shall cause voting information to be publicly posted at each polling place on the day of each election for Federal office.

(2) Voting Information Defined

In this section, the term "voting information" means—

(A) a sample version of the ballot that will be used for that election;

(B) information regarding the date of the election and the hours during which polling places will be open;

(C) instructions on how to vote, including how to cast a vote and how to cast a provisional ballot;

(D) instructions for mail-in registrants and first-time voters under section 15483(b) of this title;

(E) general information on voting rights under applicable Federal and State laws, including information on the right of an individual to cast a provisional ballot and instructions on how to contact the appropriate officials if these rights are alleged to have been violated; and

(F) general information on Federal and State laws regarding prohibitions on acts of fraud and misrepresentation.

(c) Voters Who Vote After the Polls Close

Any individual who votes in an election for Federal office as a result of a Federal or State court order or any other order extending the time established for closing the polls by a State law in effect 10 days before the date of that election may only vote in that election by casting a provisional ballot under subsection (a) of this section. Any such ballot cast under the preceding sentence shall be separated and held apart from other provisional ballots cast by those not affected by the order.

(d) Effective Date for Provisional Voting and Voting Information

Each State and jurisdiction shall be required to comply with the requirements of this section on and after January 1, 2004.

§ 15483. Computerized Statewide Voter Registration List Requirements and Requirements for Voters Who Register by Mail[227]

(a) Computerized Statewide Voter Registration List Requirements

   (1) Implementation

      (A) In General

      Except as provided in subparagraph (B), each State, acting through the chief State election official, shall implement, in a uniform and nondiscriminatory manner, a single, uniform, official, centralized, interactive computerized statewide voter registration list defined, maintained, and administered at the State level that contains the name and registration information of every legally registered voter in the State and assigns a unique identifier to each legally registered voter in the State (in this subsection referred to as the "computerized list"), and includes the following:

         (i) The computerized list shall serve as the single system for storing and managing the official list of registered voters throughout the State.

         (ii) The computerized list contains the name and registration information of every legally registered voter in the State.

         (iii) Under the computerized list, a unique identifier is assigned to each legally registered voter in the State.

---

227. Section 303.

(iv) The computerized list shall be coordinated with other agency databases within the State.

(v) Any election official in the State, including any local election official, may obtain immediate electronic access to the information contained in the computerized list.

(vi) All voter registration information obtained by any local election official in the State shall be electronically entered into the computerized list on an expedited basis at the time the information is provided to the local official.

(vii) The chief State election official shall provide such support as may be required so that local election officials are able to enter information as described in clause (vi).

(viii) The computerized list shall serve as the official voter registration list for the conduct of all elections for Federal office in the State.

(B) Exception

The requirement under subparagraph (A) shall not apply to a State in which, under a State law in effect continuously on and after October 29, 2002, there is no voter registration requirement for individuals in the State with respect to elections for Federal office.

(2) Computerized List Maintenance

(A) In General

The appropriate State or local election official shall perform list maintenance with respect to the computerized list on a regular basis as follows:

(i) If an individual is to be removed from the computerized list, such individual shall be removed in accordance with the provisions of the National Voter Registration Act of 1993 (42 U.S.C. 1973gg et seq.), including subsections (a)(4), (c)(2), (d), and (e) of section 8 of such Act (42 U.S.C. 1973gg–6).

(ii) For purposes of removing names of ineligible voters from the official list of eligible voters—

(I) under section 8(a)(3)(B) of such Act (42 U.S.C. 1973gg–6(a)(3)(B)), the State shall coordinate the computerized list with State agency records on felony status; and

(II) by reason of the death of the registrant under section 8(a)(4)(A) of such Act (42 U.S.C. 1973gg–6(a)(4)(A)), the State shall coordinate the computerized list with State agency records on death.

(iii) Notwithstanding the preceding provisions of this subparagraph, if a State is described in section 4(b) of the National Voter Registration Act of 1993 (42 U.S.C. 1973gg–2(b)), that State shall remove the names of ineligible voters from the computerized list in accordance with State law.

(B) Conduct

The list maintenance performed under subparagraph (A) shall be conducted in a manner that ensures that—

(i) the name of each registered voter appears in the computerized list;

(ii) only voters who are not registered or who are not eligible to vote are removed from the computerized list; and

(iii) duplicate names are eliminated from the computerized list.

(3) Technological Security of Computerized List

The appropriate State or local official shall provide adequate technological security measures to prevent the unauthorized access to the computerized list established under this section.

(4) Minimum Standard for Accuracy of State Voter Registration Records

The State election system shall include provisions to ensure that voter registration records in the State are accurate and are updated regularly, including the following:

(A) A system of file maintenance that makes a reasonable effort to remove registrants who are ineligible to vote from the official list of eligible voters. Under such system, consistent with the National Voter Registration Act of 1993 (42

U.S.C. 1973gg et seq.), registrants who have not responded to a notice and who have not voted in 2 consecutive general elections for Federal office shall be removed from the official list of eligible voters, except that no registrant may be removed solely by reason of a failure to vote.

(B) Safeguards to ensure that eligible voters are not removed in error from the official list of eligible voters.

(5) Verification of Voter Registration Information

(A) Requiring provision of certain information by applicants

(i) In General

Except as provided in clause (ii), notwithstanding any other provision of law, an application for voter registration for an election for Federal office may not be accepted or processed by a State unless the application includes—

(I) in the case of an applicant who has been issued a current and valid driver's license, the applicant's driver's license number; or

(II) in the case of any other applicant (other than an applicant to whom clause (ii) applies), the last 4 digits of the applicant's Social Security Number.

(ii) Special Rule for Applicants Without Driver's License or Social Security Number

If an applicant for voter registration for an election for Federal office has not been issued a current and valid driver's license or a Social Security Number, the State shall assign the applicant a number which will serve to identify the applicant for voter registration purposes. To the extent that the State has a computerized list in effect under this subsection and the list assigns unique identifying numbers to registrants, the number assigned under this clause shall be the unique identifying number assigned under the list.

(iii) Determination of Validity of Numbers Provided

The State shall determine whether the information provided by an individual is sufficient to meet the requirements of this subparagraph, in accordance with State law.

(B) Requirements for State Officials

(i) Sharing Information in Databases

The chief State election official and the official responsible for the State motor vehicle authority of a State shall enter into an agreement to match information in the database of the statewide voter registration system with information in the database of the motor vehicle authority to the extent required to enable each such official to verify the accuracy of the information provided on applications for voter registration.

(ii) Agreements with Commissioner of Social Security

The official responsible for the State motor vehicle authority shall enter into an agreement with the Commissioner of Social Security under section 405(r)(8) of this title (as added by subparagraph (C)).

[(C) omitted]

(D) Special Rule for Certain States

In the case of a State which is permitted to use Social Security Numbers, and provides for the use of Social Security Numbers, on applications for voter registration, in accordance with section 7 of the Privacy Act of 1974 (5 U.S.C. 552a note), the provisions of this paragraph shall be optional.

(b) Requirements for Voters Who Register by Mail

(1) In General

Notwithstanding section 6(c) of the National Voter Registration Act of 1993 (42 U.S.C. 1973gg–4(c)) and subject to paragraph (3), a State shall, in a uniform and nondiscriminatory manner, require an individual to meet the requirements of paragraph (2) if—

 (A) the individual registered to vote in a jurisdiction by mail; and

(B) (i) the individual has not previously voted in an election for Federal office in the State; or

(ii) the individual has not previously voted in such an election in the jurisdiction and the jurisdiction is located in a State that does not have a computerized list that complies with the requirements of subsection (a) of this section.

(2) Requirements

(A) In General

An individual meets the requirements of this paragraph if the individual—

(i) in the case of an individual who votes in person—

(I) presents to the appropriate State or local election official a current and valid photo identification; or

(II) presents to the appropriate State or local election official a copy of a current utility bill, bank statement, government check, paycheck, or other government document that shows the name and address of the voter; or

(ii) in the case of an individual who votes by mail, submits with the ballot—

(I) a copy of a current and valid photo identification; or

(II) a copy of a current utility bill, bank statement, government check, paycheck, or other government document that shows the name and address of the voter.

(B) Fail-Safe Voting

(i) In Person

An individual who desires to vote in person, but who does not meet the requirements of subparagraph (A)(i), may cast a provisional ballot under section 15482(a) of this title.

(ii) By Mail

An individual who desires to vote by mail but who does not meet the requirements of subparagraph (A)(ii) may cast such a ballot by mail and the ballot shall be counted as a provisional ballot in accordance with section 15482(a) of this title.

(3) Inapplicability

Paragraph (1) shall not apply in the case of a person—

(A) who registers to vote by mail under section 6 of the National Voter Registration Act of 1993 (42 U.S.C. 1973gg–4) and submits as part of such registration either—

(i) a copy of a current and valid photo identification; or

(ii) a copy of a current utility bill, bank statement, government check, paycheck, or government document that shows the name and address of the voter;

(B) (i) who registers to vote by mail under section 6 of the National Voter Registration Act of 1993 (42 U.S.C. 1973gg–4) and submits with such registration either—

(I) a driver's license number; or

(II) at least the last 4 digits of the individual's Social Security Number; and

(ii) with respect to whom a State or local election official matches the information submitted under clause (i) with an existing State identification record bearing the same number, name and date of birth as provided in such registration; or

(C) who is—

(i) entitled to vote by absentee ballot under the Uniformed and Overseas Citizens Absentee Voting Act [42 U.S.C. 1973ff et seq.];

(ii) provided the right to vote otherwise than in person under section 1973ee–1(b)(2)(B)(ii) of this title; or

(iii) entitled to vote otherwise than in person under any other Federal law.

(4) Contents of Mail-In Registration Form

(A) In General

The mail voter registration form developed under section 6 of the National Voter Registration Act of 1993 (42 U.S.C. 1973gg–4) shall include the following:

(i) The question "Are you a citizen of the United States of America?" and boxes for the applicant to check to indicate whether the applicant is or is not a citizen of the United States.

(ii) The question "Will you be 18 years of age on or before election day?" and boxes for the applicant to check to indicate whether or not the applicant will be 18 years of age or older on election day.

(iii) The statement "If you checked 'no' in response to either of these questions, do not complete this form."

(iv) A statement informing the individual that if the form is submitted by mail and the individual is registering for the first time, the appropriate information required under this section must be submitted with the mail-in registration form in order to avoid the additional identification requirements upon voting for the first time.

(B) Incomplete Forms

If an applicant for voter registration fails to answer the question included on the mail voter registration form pursuant to subparagraph (A)(i), the registrar shall notify the applicant of the failure and provide the applicant with an opportunity to complete the form in a timely manner to allow for the completion of the registration form prior to the next election for Federal office (subject to State law).

(5) Construction

Nothing in this subsection shall be construed to require a State that was not required to comply with a provision of the National Voter Registration Act of 1993 (42 U.S.C. 1973gg et seq.) before October 29, 2002, to comply with such a provision after October 29, 2002.

(c) Permitted Use of Last 4 Digits of Social Security Numbers

The last 4 digits of a Social Security Number described in subsections (a)(5)(A)(i)(II) and (b)(3)(B)(i)(II) of this section shall not be considered to be a Social Security Number for purposes of section 7 of the Privacy Act of 1974 (5 U.S.C. 552a note).

(d) Effective Date

(1) Computerized statewide voter registration list requirements

(A) In General

Except as provided in subparagraph (B), each State and jurisdiction shall be required to comply with the requirements of subsection (a) of this section on and after January 1, 2004.

(B) Waiver

If a State or jurisdiction certifies to the Commission not later than January 1, 2004, that the State or jurisdiction will not meet the deadline described in subparagraph (A) for good cause and includes in the certification the reasons for the failure to meet such deadline, subparagraph (A) shall apply to the State or jurisdiction as if the reference in such subparagraph to "January 1, 2004" were a reference to "January 1, 2006".

(2) *Requirement for Voters Who Register by Mail*

(A) In General

Each State and jurisdiction shall be required to comply with the requirements of subsection (b) of this section on and after January 1, 2004, and shall be prepared to receive registration materials submitted by individuals described in subparagraph (B) on and after the date described in such subparagraph.

(B) Applicability with Respect to Individuals

The provisions of subsection (b) of this section shall apply to any individual who registers to vote on or after January 1, 2003.

§ 15484. Minimum Requirements

The requirements established by this subchapter are minimum requirements and nothing in this subchapter shall be construed to prevent a State from establishing election technology and administration requirements that are more strict than the requirements established under this subchapter so long as such State requirements are not inconsistent with the Federal requirements under this subchapter or any law described in section 15545 of this title.

§ 15485. Methods of Implementation Left to Discretion of State

The specific choices on the methods of complying with the requirements of this subchapter shall be left to the discretion of the State.

Part B—Voluntary Guidance

§ 15501. Adoption of Voluntary Guidance by Commission

(a) In General

To assist States in meeting the requirements of part A of this subchapter, the Commission shall adopt voluntary guidance consistent with such requirements in accordance with the procedures described in section 15502 of this title.

(b) Deadlines

The Commission shall adopt the recommendations under this section not later than—

> (1) in the case of the recommendations with respect to section 15481 of this title, January 1, 2004;
>
> (2) in the case of the recommendations with respect to section 15482 of this title, October 1, 2003; and
>
> (3) in the case of the recommendations with respect to section 15483 of this title, October 1, 2003.

(c) Quadrennial Update

The Commission shall review and update recommendations adopted with respect to section 15481 of this title no less frequently than once every 4 years.

§ 15502. Process for Adoption

The adoption of the voluntary guidance under this part shall be carried out by the Commission in a manner that provides for each of the following:

> (1) Publication of notice of the proposed recommendations in the Federal Register.
>
> (2) An opportunity for public comment on the proposed recommendations.
>
> (3) An opportunity for a public hearing on the record.
>
> (4) Publication of the final recommendations in the Federal Register.

Subchapter IV—Enforcement

§ 15511. Actions by the Attorney General for Declaratory and Injunctive Relief

The Attorney General may bring a civil action against any State or jurisdiction in an appropriate United States District Court for such declaratory and injunctive relief (including a temporary restraining order, a permanent or temporary injunction, or other order) as may be necessary to carry out the uniform and nondiscriminatory election technology and administration requirements under sections 15481, 15482, and 15483 of this title.

§ 15512. Establishment of State-Based Administrative Complaint Procedures to Remedy Grievances

(a) Establishment of State-Based Administrative Complaint Procedures to Remedy Grievances

(1) Establishment of Procedures as Condition of Receiving Funds

If a State receives any payment under a program under this chapter, the State shall be required to establish and maintain State-based administrative complaint procedures which meet the requirements of paragraph (2).

(2) Requirements for Procedures

The requirements of this paragraph are as follows:

(A) The procedures shall be uniform and nondiscriminatory.

(B) Under the procedures, any person who believes that there is a violation of any provision of subchapter III of this chapter (including a violation which has occurred, is occurring, or is about to occur) may file a complaint.

(C) Any complaint filed under the procedures shall be in writing and notarized, and signed and sworn by the person filing the complaint.

(D) The State may consolidate complaints filed under subparagraph (B).

(E) At the request of the complainant, there shall be a hearing on the record.

(F) If, under the procedures, the State determines that there is a violation of any provision of subchapter III of this chapter, the State shall provide the appropriate remedy.

(G) If, under the procedures, the State determines that there is no violation, the State shall dismiss the complaint and publish the results of the procedures.

(H) The State shall make a final determination with respect to a complaint prior to the expiration of the 90-day period which begins on the date the complaint is filed, unless the complainant consents to a longer period for making such a determination.

(I) If the State fails to meet the deadline applicable under subparagraph (H), the complaint shall be resolved within 60 days under alternative dispute resolution procedures established for purposes of this section. The record and other materials from any proceedings conducted under the complaint procedures established under this section shall be made available for use under the alternative dispute resolution procedures.

(b) Requiring Attorney General Approval of Compliance Plan for States Not Receiving Funds

(1) In General

Not later than January 1, 2004, each nonparticipating State shall elect—

(A) to certify to the Commission that the State meets the requirements of subsection (a) of this section in the same manner as a State receiving a payment under this chapter; or

(B) to submit a compliance plan to the Attorney General which provides detailed information on the steps the State will take to ensure that it meets the requirements of subchapter III of this chapter.

(2) States Without Approved Plan Deemed Out of Compliance

A nonparticipating State (other than a State which makes the election described in paragraph (1)(A)) shall be deemed to not meet the requirements of subchapter III of this chapter if the Attorney General has not approved a compliance plan submitted by the State under this subsection.

(3) Nonparticipating State Defined

In this section, a "nonparticipating State" is a State which, during 2003, does not notify any office which is responsible for making payments to States under any program under this chapter of its intent to participate in, and receive funds under, the program.

Subchapter V—Help America Vote College Program
§ 15521. Establishment of Program
(a) In General

Not later than 1 year after the appointment of its members, the Election Assistance Commission shall develop a program to be known as the "Help America Vote College Program" (hereafter in this subchapter referred to as the "Program").

(b) Purposes of Program

The purpose of the Program shall be—

(1) to encourage students enrolled at institutions of higher education (including community colleges) to assist State and local governments in the administration of elections by serving as nonpartisan poll workers or assistants; and

(2) to encourage State and local governments to use the services of the students participating in the Program.

§ 15522. Activities Under Program
(a) In General

In carrying out the Program, the Commission (in consultation with the chief election official of each State) shall develop materials, sponsor seminars and workshops, engage in advertising targeted at students, make grants, and take such other actions as it considers appropriate to meet the purposes described in section 15521(b) of this title.

(b) Requirements for Grant Recipients

In making grants under the Program, the Commission shall ensure that the funds provided are spent for projects and activities which are carried out without partisan bias or without promoting any particular point of view regarding any issue, and that each recipient is governed in a balanced manner which does not reflect any partisan bias.

(c) Coordination with Institutions of Higher Education

The Commission shall encourage institutions of higher education (including community colleges) to participate in the Program, and shall make all necessary materials and other assistance (including materials and assistance to enable the institution to hold workshops and poll worker training sessions) available without charge to any institution which desires to participate in the Program.

§ 15523. Authorization of Appropriations

In addition to any funds authorized to be appropriated to the Commission under section 15330 of this title, there are authorized to be appropriated to carry out this subchapter—

(1) $5,000,000 for fiscal year 2003; and
(2) such sums as may be necessary for each succeeding fiscal year.

Subchapter VI—Transfer to Commission of Functions Under Certain Laws

§ 15531. Transfer of functions of Office of Election

Administration of Federal Election Commission There are transferred to the Election Assistance Commission established under section 15321 of this title all functions which the Office of Election Administration, established within the Federal Election Commission, exercised before October 29, 2002.

§ 15532. Transfer of Functions

There are transferred to the Election Assistance Commission established under section 15321 of this title all functions which the Federal Election Commission exercised under section 1973gg–7(a) of this title before October 29, 2002.

§ 15533. Transfer of Property, Records, and Personnel

(a) Property and Records

The contracts, liabilities, records, property, and other assets and interests of, or made available in connection with, the offices and functions of the Federal Election Commission which are transferred by this subchapter are transferred to the Election Assistance Commission for appropriate allocation.

(b) Personnel

(1) In General

The personnel employed in connection with the offices and functions of the Federal Election Commission which are transferred by this subchapter are transferred to the Election Assistance Commission.

(2) Effect

Any full-time or part-time personnel employed in permanent positions shall not be separated or reduced in grade or compensation because of the transfer under this subsection during the 1-year period beginning on October 29, 2002.

§ 15534. Effective Date; Transition

(a) Effective Date

This subchapter and the amendments made by this subchapter shall take effect upon the appointment of all members of the Election Assistance Commission under section 15323 of this title.

(b) Transition

With the consent of the entity involved, the Election Assistance Commission is authorized to utilize the services of such officers, employees, and other personnel of the entities from which functions have been transferred to the Election Assistance Commission under this subchapter or the amendments made by this subchapter for such period of time as may reasonably be needed to facilitate the orderly transfer of such functions.

(c) No Effect on Authorities of Office of Election Administration Prior to Appointment of Members of Commission

During the period which begins on October 29, 2002, and ends on the effective date described in subsection (a) of this section, the Office of Election Administration of the Federal Election Commission shall continue to have the authority to carry out any of the functions (including the development of voluntary standards for voting systems and procedures for the certification of voting systems) which it has the authority to carry out as of October 29, 2002.

Subchapter VII—Miscellaneous Provisions

§ 15541. State defined

In this chapter, the term "State" includes the District of Columbia, the Commonwealth of Puerto Rico, Guam, American Samoa, and the United States Virgin Islands.

§ 15542. Audits and Repayment of Funds

(a) Recordkeeping Requirement

Each recipient of a grant or other payment made under this chapter shall keep such records with respect to the payment as are consistent with sound accounting principles, including records which fully disclose the amount and disposition by such recipient of funds, the total cost of the project or undertaking for which such funds are used, and the amount of that portion of the cost of the project or undertaking supplied by other sources, and such other records as will facilitate an effective audit.

(b) Audits and Examinations

(1) Audits and Examinations

Except as provided in paragraph (5), each office making a grant or other payment under this chapter, or any duly authorized representative of such office, may audit or examine any recipient of the grant or payment and shall have access for the purpose of audit and examination to any books, documents, papers, and records of the recipient which in the opinion of the entity may be related or pertinent to the grant or payment.

(2) Recipients of Assistance Subject to Provisions of Section

The provisions of this section shall apply to all recipients of grants or other payments under this chapter, whether by direct grant, cooperative agreement, or contract under this chapter or by subgrant or subcontract from primary grantees or contractors under this chapter.

(3) Mandatory Audit

In addition to audits conducted pursuant to paragraph (1), all funds provided under this chapter shall be subject to mandatory audit by the Comptroller General at least once during the lifetime of the program involved. For purposes of an audit under this paragraph, the Comptroller General shall have access to books, documents, papers, and records of recipients of funds in the same manner as the office making the grant or payment involved has access to such books, documents, papers, and records under paragraph (1).

(4) Special Rule for Payments by General Services Administration

With respect to any grant or payment made under this chapter by the Administrator of General Services, the Election Assistance Commission shall be deemed to be the office making the grant or payment for purposes of this section.

(5) Special Rule

In the case of grants or payments made under section 15401 of this title, audits and examinations conducted under paragraph (1) shall be performed on a regular basis (as determined by the Commission).

(6) Special Rules for Audits by the Commission

In addition to the audits described in paragraph (1), the Election Assistance Commission may conduct a special audit or special examination of a recipient described in paragraph (1) upon a vote of the Commission.

(c) Recoupment of Funds

If the Comptroller General determines as a result of an audit conducted under subsection (b) of this section that—

>(1) a recipient of funds under this chapter is not in compliance with each of the requirements of the program under which the funds are provided; or

>(2) an excess payment has been made to the recipient under the program, the recipient shall pay to the office which made the grant or payment involved a portion of the funds provided which reflects the proportion of the requirements with which the recipient is not in compliance, or the extent to which the payment is in excess, under the program involved.

§ 15543. Review and Report on Adequacy of Existing Electoral Fraud Statutes and Penalties

(a) Review

The Attorney General shall conduct a review of existing criminal statutes concerning election offenses to determine—

(1) whether additional statutory offenses are needed to secure the use of the Internet for election purposes; and

(2) whether existing penalties provide adequate punishment and deterrence with respect to such offenses.

(b) Report

The Attorney General shall submit a report to the Committees on the Judiciary of the Senate and House of Representatives, the Committee on Rules and Administration of the Senate, and the Committee on House Administration of the House of Representatives on the review conducted under subsection (a) of this section together with such recommendations for legislative and administrative action as the Attorney General determines appropriate.

§ 15544. Other Criminal Penalties

(a) Conspiracy to Deprive Voters of a Fair Election

Any individual who knowingly and willfully gives false information in registering or voting in violation of section 1973i(c) of this title, or conspires with another to violate such section, shall be fined or imprisoned, or both, in accordance with such section.

(b) False Information in Registering and Voting

Any individual who knowingly commits fraud or knowingly makes a false statement with respect to the naturalization, citizenry, or alien registry of such individual in violation of section 1015 of title 18 shall be fined or imprisoned, or both, in accordance with such section.

§ 15545. No Effect on Other Laws

(a) In General

Except as specifically provided in section 15483(b) of this title with regard to the National Voter Registration Act of 1993 (42 U.S.C. 1973gg et seq.), nothing in this chapter may be construed to authorize or require conduct prohibited under any of the following laws, or to supersede, restrict, or limit the application of such laws:

The Help America Vote Act

(1) The Voting Rights Act of 1965 (42 U.S.C. 1973 et seq.).

(2) The Voting Accessibility for the Elderly and Handicapped Act (42 U.S.C. 1973ee et seq.).

(3) The Uniformed and Overseas Citizens Absentee Voting Act (42 U.S.C. 1973ff et seq.).

(4) The National Voter Registration Act of 1993 (42 U.S.C. 1973gg et seq.).

(5) The Americans with Disabilities Act of 1990 (42 U.S.C. 12101 et seq.).

(6) The Rehabilitation Act of 1973 (29 U.S.C. 701 et seq.).

(b) No Effect on Preclearance or Other Requirements Under Voting Rights Act

The approval by the Administrator or the Commission of a payment or grant application under subchapter I or subchapter II of this chapter, or any other action taken by the Commission or a State under such subchapter, shall not be considered to have any effect on requirements for preclearance under section 5 of the Voting Rights Act of 1965 (42 U.S.C. 1973c) or any other requirements of such Act [42 U.S.C. 1973 et seq.].

The Federal Judicial Center

Board

The Chief Justice of the United States, *Chair*
Judge Catherine Blake, U.S. District Court for the District of Maryland
Magistrate Judge John Michael Facciola, U.S. District Court for the District of Columbia
Judge James B. Haines Jr., U.S. Bankruptcy Court for the District Maine
Judge James F. Holderman Jr., U.S. District Court for the Northern District of Illinois
Judge Michael Melloy, U.S. Court of Appeals for the Eighth Circuit
Judge Edward C. Prado, U.S. Court of Appeals for the Fifth Circuit
Judge Kathryn H. Vratil, U.S. District Court for the District of Kansas
Judge Thomas F. Hogan, Director of the Administrative Office of the U.S. Courts

Director
Judge Jeremy D. Fogel

Deputy Director
John S. Cooke

About the Federal Judicial Center

The Federal Judicial Center is the research and education agency of the federal judicial system. It was established by Congress in 1967 (28 U.S.C. §§ 620–629), on the recommendation of the Judicial Conference of the United States.

By statute, the Chief Justice of the United States chairs the Center's Board, which also includes the director of the Administrative Office of the U.S. Courts and seven judges elected by the Judicial Conference.

The organization of the Center reflects its primary statutory mandates. The Education Division plans and produces education and training programs for judges and court staff, including satellite broadcasts, video programs, publications, curriculum packages for in-court training, and Web-based programs and resources. The Research Division examines and evaluates current and alternative federal court practices and policies. This research assists Judicial Conference committees, who request most Center research, in developing policy recommendations. The Center's research also contributes substantially to its educational programs. The two divisions work closely with two units of the Director's Office—the Information Technology Office and Communications Policy & Design Office—in using print, broadcast, and on-line media to deliver education and training and to disseminate the results of Center research. The Federal Judicial History Office helps courts and others study and preserve federal judicial history. The International Judicial Relations Office provides information to judicial and legal officials from foreign countries and assesses how to inform federal judicial personnel of developments in international law and other court systems that may affect their work.

www.ingramcontent.com/pod-product-compliance
Lightning Source LLC
Chambersburg PA
CBHW070040210526
45170CB00012B/553